HAZEL *Blomkamp*

Crewel
birds

Jacobean embroidery takes flight

HAZEL *Blomkamp*

Crewel
birds

Jacobean embroidery takes flight

SEARCH PRESS

ACKNOWLEDGEMENTS & THANKS

Thank you to Margie Breetzke, Louise Grimbeek, Pat Burchell, Alexandra Cullen and Carol Pay who together make up a team of proof stitchers. They have stitched every single one of these birds, picking up mistakes I have made and burning the midnight oil to stitch through the designs in time for publication.

Pat van Wyk for devising and making up the rag book of birds.

Thank you also to all at Metz Press. You are fabulous publishers and it is always a pleasure to work with you.

First published in Great Britain in 2020 by
Search Press Limited
Wellwood, North Farm Road,
Tunbridge Wells, Kent, TN2 3DR

Originally published in South Africa in 2020 by
Metz Press, 1 Cameronians Ave, Welgemoed
7530, South Africa

ISBN 978-1-78221-834-0

Suppliers
If you have difficulty in obtaining any of the
materials and equipment mentioned in this
book, then please visit the Search Press website
for details of suppliers: www.searchpress.com

Publisher   Wilsia Metz
Design   Liezl Maree
Lay-out   Lindie Metz
Proofreader   Nikki Metz
Illustrations   Hazel Blomkamp
Photographer   Kenny Irvine

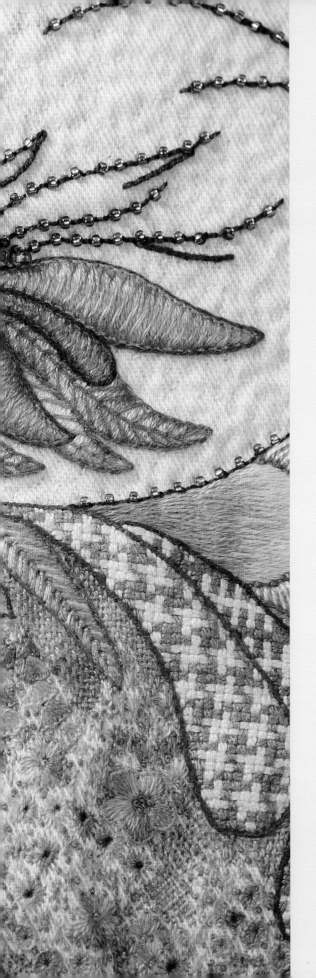

Contents

Introduction

When I was working on the two birds in my last book, I kept thinking of the many different birds that are to be found in our natural world and, having enjoyed designing and stitching those birds, I decided that a book of birds would be a wonderful journey. The only problem was to choose which birds to depict because there is so much diversity with so much choice.

I pondered poultry, tropical birds, little twittery birds that sing outside my bedroom window in the morning or more traditional Jacobean-style fanciful birds. I eventually settled on a mix of the larger birds and in this book, you will find:

Claude the Fanciful Phoenix. This bird is my take on traditional depictions of the phoenix or firebird with the slightly unusual colours deriving from nothing more curious than the fact that there were some colours in my thread box that I really wanted to play with.

Colin the Rooster. In every country of the world people keep poultry and every fowl run has a rooster. This bird is no specific breed of fowl but rather a combination of the colours that are to be found across the breeds.

Dave the Pheasant. This is a fanciful depiction of the common pheasant which many would think is the least interesting of the breed. I don't think so. Our local veterinary surgery has a slightly crippled specimen in the aviary where they feed and care for birds that won't cope in the wild. Every time I go in there, I admire its colouring, particularly in the sunlight. I needed to interpret those colours in thread.

Kevin the Fanciful Pheasant. Based on traditional pheasant designs to be found in Chinese art, on porcelain and in crewel embroidery, Kevin is a colourful and flowery version of this bird.

Dick the Duck. Of all the breeds of ducks to be found in the world, the mallard is the most interesting because of its colours. About to take flight, this duck has the most diverse techniques and stitches in this book.

Nigel the Flamingo. I could not resist the challenge of working with the colours of the pink flamingo - a mix of oranges and pinks. I had a lot of fun with this chap.

Like so many artists that have stitched for decades, my walls are full of framed pictures. There is no space for anything more. Therefore, I decided to bind all of these birds into what I will loosely call a 'rag book'. All of the projects are approximately the same size and I have hand quilted them with batting and a backing. Pat van Wyk, an amazing quilter and wonderful friend, has finished them off for me with a spine and binding to create this rag book. With her guidance, I have provided the instructions for making this book in the chapter on general project instructions.

You might choose to do the same but if you don't, every one of the projects would be suitable for framing, cushions, quilt panels, whatever you choose to make from them.

Because it is the male birds that have the most appealing plumage, these birds had to be given boys' names. Following on from what I started in my *Crewel Creatures* book, I have named these birds after male dogs that I have had in my life, or puppies that I have bred in recent years - puppies that went off to fabulous homes and were given different names. Yes, I did have a dog called Dick. He was a beautiful boxer who lived up to his name in spectacular fashion. He was always being borrowed for stud purposes. By naming my projects after these dogs, I am honouring each and every one of them for the precious part that they have played in my life.

Whether you work the projects in this book, or you use the techniques that I have used in your own embroidery projects, I hope you will find value in what I have enjoyed putting together in this publication.

HAZEL *Blomkamp*

Tips before starting

YOU MUST BE ABLE TO SEE PROPERLY

One of the most common inhibiting factors for embroiderers, especially those of a certain age and older, is being able to see properly. This is of importance when one is doing fine work and there is a lot of that in this book.

Optometrists' machines are set to magnify at about waist level. This does not work for embroidery because you will generally hold your work at chest level. When you visit your optometrist, take a piece of your work with you so that your spectacles can be made to suit your working style.

The best spectacles are multi-focals with a small spot in the bottom part of the lenses made to magnify, by two or three times, at chest level. Alternatively, you can have your optometrist make you a dedicated pair of spectacles for needlework. I have a pair of those and they're not pretty. The lenses are so thick that they look like the bottoms of whisky glasses. So what. They work and that's the main thing.

There are times, though, when even those are not enough and that is when I put on a second pair. That is, a pair of +1.5 readers in front of the whisky glasses. This creates a telescope and is more comfortable than grappling with one of those magnifying glasses that hang around your neck, or craning your neck to look through a beauticians' magnifying light. If you are travelling, this system works very well as there is so little to take with you.

Good light

You don't want to have to restrict yourself to only being able to work during daylight hours, so you will need a good light or lights. Over the years I've tried just about every single lighting system out there and have now gone back to basics. Two inexpensive metal angle-poise lamps fitted with 15-watt energy-saving bulbs. They are set up on either side of me as I stitch. Because they are angle-poise, I pull them closer or push them away depending on what I am stitching. This really is the best lighting system for me.

And here's the thing. My life is filled with mad and crazy big dogs that knock things over. If they destroy either of these very affordable lights it doesn't hurt quite so much when I have to buy a replacement.

HOOPS AND FRAMES

I reject so-called rules when it comes to any kind of creativity. I do think, though, that if there has to be any single rule for embroidery, it is that you must work in a hoop or frame. It improves the tension of your work and for many of the techniques it prevents the fabric from puckering. You cannot produce good work without them.

The projects in this book use 17 x 17" stretcher bars.

FABRIC GUARDS

No matter how often you wash your hands, or how clean you keep your working environment, a grubby ring is likely to form at the place where the fabric meets the outer ring of the hoop. To avoid this problem, make a fabric guard.

Measure the circumference or outside measurement of your hoop or frame. Add 50 mm (2") for a small hoop and 100 mm (4") for a large hoop or frame. Using that measurement, cut a strip of fabric that is 250 mm (10") wide.

Fold the strip in half, with right sides together, and sew a seam to join the ends of the strip, making it into a tube.

Stitch a 15 mm (⅝") casing by turning in a hem at top and bottom.

Calculate how much narrow elastic you will need by tightly stretching a piece around the circumference or outside of the hoop or frame, adding 25 mm (1"). Cut two pieces and thread them into the top and bottom casings, stitch them together and close the gaps of the casings.

Once you have stretched the working fabric into the hoop, stretch the fabric guard around the perimeter of the hoop, protecting the edge of the embroidery, and tucking the excess working fabric on the outside of the hoop into the part of the fabric guard the lies below the hoop.

USE A THREAD CONDITIONER

Beeswax is good, but the best is a silicone thread conditioner. This leaves no residue. It strengthens your thread, makes silk and rayon threads less lively and delays the stripping of metallic thread. It certainly prevents tangles and knotting when you are working with long pieces of beading thread.

THE WONDERS OF SUPERGLUE

I don't like using a thimble but find that a hole develops in the tip of the finger that I use to push the needle through the fabric, particularly with hand-quilting through layers in the projects in this book. It is very sore if I happen to push the needle on that spot which, inevitably I always do. I place a blob of superglue on the pad of my middle finger and hold it in the air for a few minutes. Once that blob is dry it will be rock hard and a needle will not penetrate it. It peels off after a few hours. Ignore the neurotics who predict dire health problems. They're wrong. I've used it for years and I've never had to go to the emergency room.

START AND END THREADS WITH A KNOT

We do needlework for our pleasure, not to be judged. Whilst the back of your work should not look like a bird's nest, it does not have to look the same as the front. It really doesn't. This is the 21st century.

THE STITCHES IN THIS BOOK

Like all girls of my generation, I learnt embroidery at school and from older members of my family. Since then I have developed in my own way, working stitches and techniques to achieve the look I want as opposed to conforming to what somebody else tells me I should be doing. The way that I have worked the stitches and the techniques in this book are illustrated and described in the techniques' galleries. If you have been taught or have learnt differently, you should use the way that works best for you. This applies, in particular, to long and short stitch shading. Do each stitch in a way that works best for you.

If you are unsure of any of the stitches, practise on a scrap of fabric with scrap thread before working on the project. Don't use thread from the list provided for each project as you might run out of those threads.

SLOW AND METHODICAL IS BEST

Remember that we do needlework for pleasure. I enjoy the journey that is each design I stitch and when I reach my destination I am often bereft.

Focus on the pleasure of working each square inch, aiming for it to be as perfect as you can possibly make it. If a stitch is not sitting at the right angle, take it out before you move on. The same applies to beads. If you don't do that, others may not notice but you will. Every time you look at it.

Enjoy watching each part come alive before your eyes.

WASHING YOUR EMBROIDERY

We are living in the 21st century with good dyes and non-shrinking fabrics. So you can wash your needle work. Provided you have checked that all the dyes are colourfast – which they should be if you have used good quality thread – you must wash it. It brings the colours to life and the sheen of the thread reappears.

- Rinse it well in cold water to get rid of any lines that you may have drawn with a washout pen.
- Soak it for a few hours in tepid water mixed with a tablespoon or two of good detergent.
- Swish it around a bit before rinsing it in cold water. If you find there are marks – perhaps chalk paper lines – that haven't washed out, scrub them gently with pure soap on a tooth-brush.
- Rinse again to make sure that no soap or detergent remains.
- Squeeze out the excess water, place it flat on a towel and roll up the towel.
- Squeeze the towel with the embroidery inside it to get rid of any remaining excess water.
- Stretch the damp embroidery in a hoop or frame that is larger than the embroidered area and place it in front of an open window, out of direct sunlight, to dry in the breeze.
- If you have stretched it well you will probably not need to iron it when it is dry. If you do need to iron it, turn it wrong side up on a folded towel and press the back with an iron set on medium heat.

Materials and tools

FABRICS

I have chosen to work on the fabrics described here. You may choose to work on a different colour or a different fabric. My preference is for fabric that comprises natural fibres, but for your project it will be your choice. The rule of thumb is only that the fabric should be stable, washable and strong enough to accommodate the stitches and beadwork. Although unlikely to shrink, it is always wise to rinse all fabrics in cold water before you use them. Once it is dry and pressed, cut your fabric to the required size.

200 gsm 45/55 linen-cotton blend

The rooster, pheasant, duck and flamingo in this book have been worked on a natural-coloured 200 gsm 45/55 linen-cotton blend. It is a strong and stable fabric woven with natural fibres and of a weight that is suitable for soft furnishings, but is also light enough to stretch over core board for framing.

220 gsm pure cotton-twill construction

The two fanciful birds, Claude and Kevin, have been worked on what I would call a lightweight twill, colour Ecru. It has the diagonal weaving lines that you would find in twill but, whilst being strong and stable, it is suitable for soft furnishings and also light enough to stretch over core board for framing.

Cotton voile

Each project lists cotton voile backing fabric. By backing your base fabric with voile, you provide stability and give yourself a place to end off the thread. Lightweight and smooth cotton voile in white, off-white or Ecru is the perfect fabric to use. Cut a piece to the same size as the embroidery fabric, tack the two pieces together with horizontal and vertical lines through the middle and overlock or machine stitch around the edges to prevent fraying.

100 gsm polyester or cotton batting

All of the projects in this book have been quilted using Loomtex – a low-loft standard needle-punched/spray-bonded combination polyester batting. If this is not available in your country you would need to find a similar low-loft batting. It should not be too thick or luxurious because you don't want the final result to turn out too puffy. If you are quilting the project you will need an additional block of cotton voile to place behind the batting when you stretch it into the frame.

THREADS AND THEIR NEEDLES

When embroidering, you should endeavour to use quality threads. Their dyes should be colourfast, they should not break easily and should not develop fluff-balls while you are working with them. The threads used in this book are available worldwide and largely fulfil these criteria.

Any country that signed the 1997 Kyoto Protocol undertook to, amongst other things, ban certain toxic chemicals in the dyes that are used in textiles. This means that it has become impossible to guarantee colour-fastness in any fabric or thread. Whilst many thread manufacturers still claim that their threads are colourfast, this is not strictly correct, particularly with regard to the darker reds, greens and purples.

It is advisable to check all threads before use by dipping a small length into hot water then dabbing it dry on a white towel. If no colour comes out it is good to use. If colours do run then dunk the whole skein into the hot water, dabbing it dry and repeating this process until the white towel stays white.

Stranded cotton

Usually six-stranded, this thread comes in skeins of 8 m. It has a lustrous sheen and you can embroider with as many strands as you wish, depending on the texture you wish to achieve. It is ideal for fine work. This book uses stranded cotton from the DMC range. For the projects in this book, use a size 7 or 10 embroidery needle when stitching with stranded cotton.

Perle thread

This twisted thread is available in a variety of sizes and colours, with a sheen that is remarkably effective. It is easy to work with and provides alternative texture to your work. It is ideal for many of the weaving and needle-lace stitches featured. This book uses thread from the DMC perle #12 and Presencia Finca #12 or #16 ranges. Because of the twist it is inclined to tangle. To guard against this, run it through a thread conditioner. Use a size 7 embroidery, a size 26 chenille or a size 26 tapestry needle when stitching with perle thread.

Fine cordonette thread

This book uses DMC Special Dentelles 80 for the finer needle-lace and weaving stitches. Similar to perle, it is a twisted thread with a light sheen. As with perle thread, because of the twist it is inclined to tangle. To guard against this, run it through a thread conditioner. Use a size 7 embroidery or a size 26 tapestry needle when stitching with this thread.

Metallic thread

Although manufactured from polyester yarn, metallic threads have the appearance of metal and are guaranteed to add an exciting dimension to your work, particularly when used in conjunction with beads. These threads shred easily so you should work with short pieces and re-thread often. Thread conditioner provides lubrication and protection, so should be used. This book uses metallic thread from the Madeira Metallic and DMC Diamant ranges. You should use a size 7 embroidery or a size 22 chenille needle when stitching with metallic threads.

Silk ribbon

Soft and sublime, these ribbons are made from pure silk and are available in a variety of widths. This book uses 2 mm Di van Niekerk hand-painted ribbon to weave an extra dimension into some of the lace fillings. Because silk ribbon is reasonably fragile and damages easily you should work with short pieces on a size 24 or 26 tapestry needle.

BEADS AND CRYSTALS

Seed beads

When adding beads to your embroidery you should endeavour to seek out the best beads that you can find. Using inferior quality beads ruins the effect of your work. Seed beads come from many

countries and many different factories. Many of them are badly shaped, of uneven sizing and with holes that are off-centre. The best beads come from Japan and this book uses beads from the Miyuki range of Japanese seed beads.

Bead sizing is determined by the number of beads that fit into an inch which means that, like counted-thread linen, the higher the number, the smaller the bead. In this book, the projects use size 15° round rocailles and #1 (3 mm) bugle beads.

When incorporating beads into your embroidery stitches, attach them to fabric using stranded cotton, the colour of which should be similar to the shade of the bead. It is sometimes better, though, when attaching single beads, to use a thread colour that is identical to the background fabric. It can be useful, when working with transparent beads, to attach them with a completely different coloured thread. In this way, you can alter the colour of the bead to create additional shading.

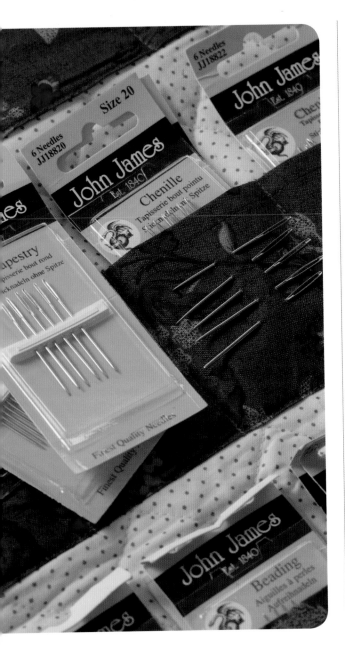

Crystals

To be called crystal, glass must use a minimum of 24% lead or metal oxide in its manufacture. The sizing of crystal rhinestones and beads is metric and indicates either the diameter or the length of the glass object. This book uses Preciosa flat-back crystals for the eyes of four of the six birds. They are perfect for creating glinting eyes that seem to look at you, even follow you. Attaching these crystals is described in the bead embroidery gallery.

CUTTING TOOLS

- Large dressmaking scissors for cutting fabric
- A rotary cutter (optional)
- Small, sharp scissors for cutting threads.

NEEDLES

- Embroidery/crewel needles, sizes 7 and 10
- Tapestry needles, sizes 24 and 26
- Quilting needles, size 11 sharps
- Short beading/bead-embroidery needles, sizes 10 or 12.

TRACING

- Dressmaker's carbon
- Alternatively, a light box for transferring designs onto fabric used in conjunction with a Pilot Frixion pen or a soft pencil.

GENERAL TOOLS

- A sewing machine and good quality thread
- Stretcher bars – two pairs 17"
- Thread conditioner
- A beading mat or beading tray
- A seam ripper or stitch cutter for unpicking
- A pair of tweezers to get rid of fluff when you are unpicking
- A spinster twisting tool for cord-making.

Because the holes in the beads are small and you will need to pass the needle through, sometimes more than once, you have the choice of using a bead-embroidery needle or a size 11 sharps needle. My preference is for the sharps needles. They are short and bend less. All these needles have an extremely small eye so you should use only one strand of thread which you then double over for extra strength.

General project instructions

Each project in this book forms the page of a rag book. I have chosen to do this because I have no space left on the walls of my house – so I would have nowhere to put them if I chose to frame them. You may choose not to do this, which will mean that preparation of the fabric and the finishing off of each project would be different. The preparation instructions below describe what I have done.

In addition, because they are all so similar, I have included general instructions for the projects below. These instructions apply to needles, threads and the finishing-off of each page of the rag book.

TRANSFERRING THE DESIGN

The line drawings for all the designs in this book are at the back. They are not the correct size, but that size is noted. You could bring them up to the correct size on a photocopier but that is never ideal. My suggestion is that you scan the drawing and set it to print at the correct size. If you are unable to do this yourself, you will find that most copy shops will be able to do it for you.

Once you have the correct size drawing, the easiest way to transfer it onto your fabric is with dressmaker's carbon. Like most things in life, I do what works best for me. And dressmaker's carbon, or chalk paper, is my choice.
• Pin the printed drawing to the fabric, taking care to place it in the centre. Don't get too fussy about the grain, just get it as straight as you can;
• Place a sheet of dressmaker's carbon, ink side down, between the photocopy and the fabric;

• Using the hard tip of a ballpoint pen (preferably one that has no ink in it – I have a dry pen in my toolbox for this task), go over each and every line, pressing hard. And I do mean pressing hard. You should end up with a sore finger. If you don't press hard enough the lines won't transfer.

Another alternative is to pin the photocopy to the underside of the fabric. Place it on a light box and trace the lines onto the fabric with a pencil or a Pilot Frixion pen.

And if the above is all too much for you, order a print pack from our website!

PENS

If you have transferred your design with chalk paper, you may find that the lines fade. This is because as you stitch, your hand rubs over those lines taking some of the chalk off every time. It is advisable to draw over those lines with a Pilot Frixion pen before you start embroidering.

The Frixion pen is fairly new on the market and I have to say that, until recently, I had resisted using it. I stuck resolutely to the blue washout pen and I was taken in by the idea that the chemicals in the ink may cause damage to the fabric a hundred years down the line. Well actually, who cares. I'm long gone by then and what is more important is that I need to use something that works well today. And this pen works very nicely, thank you. I now use it exclusively and in preference to the blue washout pen.

The lines come out when you apply heat and pressing the fabric with an iron is generally advised. I find, however, that a hair dryer works better. There are those who will tell you that the lines come back in cold temperatures and to them I will say, maybe. I did an experiment last year, did a large and messy scribble on a piece of cotton fabric with the pen. I then blew out the scribble with a hair dryer and placed the fabric in the deep freeze overnight. The next morning, I found the fabric frozen stiff but the scribble had not returned. That was all the proof I needed.

The Pilot Frixion has become my favourite pen.

PREPARATION

Back the fabric on which you have drawn the lines with a piece of cotton voile. Overlock around the four edges or, if you do not have an overlocker, tack a small hem or go around the edges with a standard sewing machine set on zig zag stitch.

You have two options when it comes to stitching the project.

If you are intending to frame the finished project, or turn it into something like a cushion, you will not want to use batting to bulk it up. If, however, you wish to turn the project into a page of a rag book, like I have done, you will need to bulk it up and quilt the fabric to the batting.

This can be done from the beginning or, if you don't want to stitch through all of the layers throughout the project, you can add the batting to the back only when you stitch the background. I did it from the beginning for all of the projects and my instructions below reflect that. All the original projects were worked on Edmunds 17" stretcher bars.

1. Cut off a strip of batting of 76 x 381 mm (3 x 15"). Reserve this for making the page of the book, described later.

2. Lay the spare piece of cotton voile over the stretcher bars followed by the remaining, large piece of batting. Place the backed and overlocked print over the batting.

3. Make sure that everything is taut, with no creases in any layer, and that you have placed them evenly. This will improve the quality of your work.

4. Secure all of the layers to the side of the stretcher bars using either thumbtacks or a staple gun, stretching all four layers as you go so that by the time you have done all four sides, the stitching area is as tight as a drum skin.

THREADS AND NEEDLES

- Assume that threads are stranded cotton unless otherwise specified.
- When working with stranded cotton, use two strands in a size 7 or 8 embroidery needle, unless otherwise advised.
- If advised to use a single strand, work with a size 10 embroidery needle.
- Work all bead-embroidery stitches with a single strand, doubled over and threaded onto a size 11 sharps quilting or a size 10 bead-embroidery needle.
- Work with a single strand of the perle and dentelles threads.
- Use a size 7 embroidery needle when you work the warp stitches in the weaving.
- Use a size 24 or 26 tapestry needle for the weft stitches in the weaving.
- Use a size 26 or 28 tapestry needle for the needle-lace detached buttonhole stitches.

FINISHING OFF

If you choose to turn your project into a rag book, as I have done, the following instructions apply.

When you have completed, or are some way to completing, the first embroidery project, pop down to your closest supplier of cotton quilting-fabric and get yourself 5 x 0,5 m (½ yd) pieces of fabric in the green/blue/turquoise range of shades. Mix and match them, making sure that they tone in with the embroidery project that you have taken with you.

Making up a page

Because quilting techniques are traditionally worked in inches – and our equipment is in inches – the following instructions use imperial measurements, with the metric conversions alongside in brackets.

Width will vary for each page according to the embroidery

1. Trim the original embroidery piece so that it measures 14" (356 mm) high.

2. Trim the left and right sides to ½" (10 mm) beyond the edge of the hand embroidery.

3. Cut a strip of quilting fabric 15" (381 mm) high. This is slightly longer than the height of the trimmed embroidery but will accommodate any shrinkage that may occur when it is quilted.

4. The width of the strip will vary on each page, depending on the width of each individual embroidery. Calculate this width so that the finished page will measure 14" (356 mm) wide, remembering to add ½" (10 mm) for the seam allowance where it is joined to the embroidery. It will do no harm to add an additional inch when calculating the width to allow for shrinkage when quilting. It can be trimmed off later.

5. Join the fabric strip to the embroidery. With right sides together and the fabric strip facing into the embroidery piece, pin and stitch the strip to the left side with a seam allowance of ½" (10 mm).

6. Cut a strip of batting 15" (381 mm) high and as

wide as necessary. Place it under the added quilting fabric so that it abuts the quilted embroidery piece. Pin it firmly and smoothly into place.

7. Without adding any additional backing, machine stitch straight lines from the top to the bottom of the strip starting ½" (10 mm) in from where you have joined it to the embroidery piece. Follow this with additional machine-stitched straight lines, from top to bottom, ½" (10 mm) apart until you have quilted the strip that now forms the spine of the page.

8. Trim the spine so that the entire page (including the embroidery piece) measures 14" (356 mm) x 14" (356 mm).

9. From your stash of quilting fabric, cut a backing for the page that also measures 14" (356 mm) x 14" (356 mm).

10. With the right side showing on the back, sandwich it to the page. Pin it into place, making sure that it is flat with no creases anywhere.

11. Place a continuous binding around the whole page following the instructions that follow.

Back and front covers

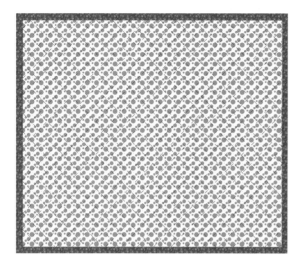

1. Cut four squares of fabric that measure 15" (381 mm) x 15" (381 mm). You don't have to use the same fabric throughout; it's quite nice to mix and match.

2. Create each cover by sandwiching one piece of fabric, a piece of batting and one more piece of fabric.

3. When quilting the sandwiched fabric block it is useful to use a walking foot, if you have one. Using a pencil, Frixion pen, or whatever washout pen you would normally use, draw a diagonal line across the middle of the block going one way and then a second diagonal line that sits at right angles to the first line.

4. Cross hatch the entire block by sewing simple diagonal lines, 1" (25 mm) apart, on your sewing machine. Do the lines that go one way first and then complete those that go in the other direction.

5. If you don't have a walking foot, draw all of the lines to guide you.

6. Once you have completed the cross hatching, trim the block to 14" (356 mm) x 14" (356 mm) and finish off each cover with continuous binding as instructed below. It is nice to choose a different, contrasting fabric for the binding.

Continuous binding

1. Cut a 3" (76 mm) strip of fabric, on the straight grain of the fabric, that is long enough to go all of the way around the bordered edge of the project, with room to spare for the corners. This will vary according to the size of the project.

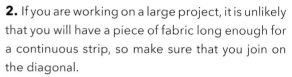

2. If you are working on a large project, it is unlikely that you will have a piece of fabric long enough for a continuous strip, so make sure that you join on the diagonal.

3. Fold the strip in half and press it with an iron, so that you end up with a long strip that is 1½" (38 mm) wide.

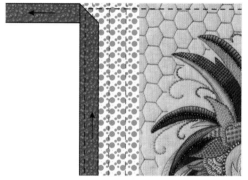

4. With the raw edge of the strip facing the outer edge and starting in the middle of the bottom border of the project, pin and stitch the strip to the end of that side. Leave 3" (76 mm) to accommodate working a diagonal join when you meet up with where you started at the end.

5. Referring to the diagram above, fold the strip to the left to create a 45° angle at the corner.

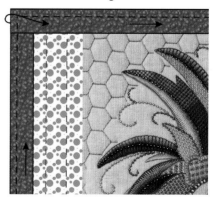

6. With the 45° angle neatly underneath, fold the fabric, at a 90° angle to the right (see the last diagram on page 24). Pin and stitch it, with raw edges to the outside, to the corresponding edge.

7. Work the remaining three corners in this way.

8. When you meet up with where you started on the bottom edge, unfold the binding, work a diagonal join, fold it in half again and complete the stitching along that edge.

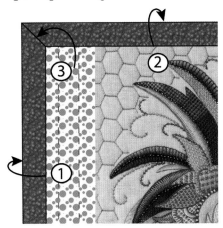

9. Referring to arrows (1) and (2) in the diagram above, turn the binding to the back of the project so that the folded edge meets up with the stitching line. Pin and hand stitch the binding on the back, your stitching corresponding to that stitching line on the back.

10. A mitre will have formed on each corner.

11. Where they meet up, as depicted by arrow 3 in the diagram, slip-stitch the two ends of the binding together.

Assembling your rag book

1. You will need six decorative or plain buttons, of a diameter of at least 25 mm (1"), that match the colouring of the front and back covers.

2. When you have completed each page and both covers, pile them on top of one another in the order that you would like them to be displayed. Make sure that they are properly lined up.

3. Choose a thick needle from your collection, the only guideline being that it should fit through the holes in the buttons. Mattress and carpet needles are too thick. I used a size 5 hand-sewing needle and, if the truth be told, it was very bent by the time I had completed the job. But it didn't break and that was the important thing.

4. Mark the spot where you wish to put each button – they should be evenly spaced, three on the front and three on the back – and thread unbreakable thread onto the needle. I used a two-ply beading thread.

5. With a knot at the tail end of the thread, come up from the back to the front.

6. Pick up the first button, going through one of the holes. Go down through the second hole in the button, take the needle to the back, picking up the first button for the back by going through one of the holes. Go up through the second hole in that button, take the needle to the front, going through the first hole in the button that is already in place. Keep going in this way, stitching both buttons on at the same time, until you have done enough stitches to make it secure.

7. End off by securing the thread under the back button. Attach the remaining buttons in the same way.

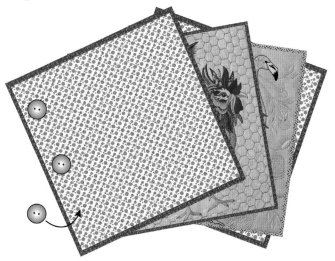

Stitches and techniques

Embroidery stitches

Backstitch

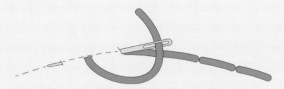

Working from right to left, bring the needle up a stitch length before the end of the line you wish to stitch. Go in at the end of the line, coming up again a stitch length away from the beginning of the stitch you are working. Repeat as necessary, keeping your stitch length as even as possible.

Backstitch – interlaced

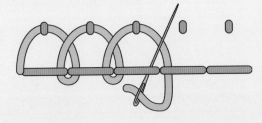

Referring to the pink lines in the diagram, bring your needle up a stitch length away from the end of the line you wish to stitch. Go in at the end of the line, coming up on the outline of the shape approximately opposite the middle of the backstitch. Work a small, straight stitch at right angles to the backstitch. Come up a stitch length away from the beginning of the last backstitch, on the backstitch line. Go into the same hole that you came out of when you started the first backstitch. Before moving onto the next backstitch, work the straight stitch at right angles and opposite the middle

of the working backstitch. When you have completed the line of backstitch and straight stitches, possibly changing to a contrasting thread, come up at the start of the backstitch line. Go under the straight stitch on the side and under the second backstitch. Changing direction, go under the first backstitch and under the next straight stitch on the side. Keep going in this way until all the backstitches have been laced.

Backstitch – split

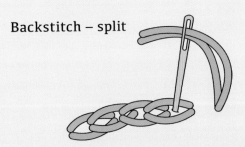

This is easier to work and gives a more pleasing result than traditional split stitch. Work a backstitch using two strands of thread. Come up further along the line and instead of going back into the hole at the end of the first stitch as you would for normal backstitch, take the needle down between the two threads of the previous backstitch, making sure that the threads of that stitch lie side by side with no twists. Keep going in this way.

Backstitch – whipped

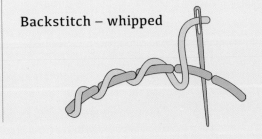

It is advisable to use a tapestry needle when whipping. To whip backstitch, bring your needle up adjacent to the beginning of the line of stitching. Take your needle and thread over, then under each stitch. A contrasting colour thread is often effective.

Backstitch/French knot combination

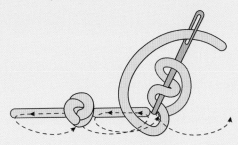

Working from right to left, bring the needle up a stitch length before the end of the line you wish to stitch. Go in at the end of the line, coming up again in the hole at the beginning of the first backstitch. Work a French knot, going back into approximately the same hole at the beginning of the backstitch. Bring the needle up a stitch length further along the line to create the next backstitch which you complete by going into the fabric under the French knot – more or less into the same hole. Come up at the beginning of the present backstitch to create the next French knot and keep going in this way.

Battlement couching

Starting with the darkest colour, work a layer of long straight stitches across the area. These can be vertical or diagonal and you should leave enough space between them to accommodate two or three more layers and a space between the blocks when they have been completed. Work another layer of long straight stitches that are placed at right angles to the first layer. Work one or two more layers in different shades of thread. It is important to work in the same order for all of the layers of straight stitches so that you get a woven effect where the stitches intersect. Finally, work small, straight couching stitches over the intersection of the last layer of trellis stitches.

Blanket and buttonhole stitch

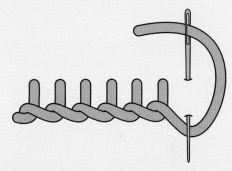

These two stitches are formed in the same way. The difference between the two is that buttonhole stitches are placed close together whilst blanket stitches have gaps between them. Working from left to right, bring the needle up on the bottom edge where you require the ridge. Take the needle in at the top edge and out again at the bottom edge, with the thread looped under the needle. Pull through and repeat as required. Secure at the end with a small couching stitch over the last one at the ridge edge.

Blanket stitch – double

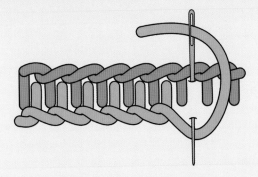

Work a line of blanket stitch (see page 27) leaving a small space between the stitches. When you have completed the row, turn the work around and work a line of blanket stitch that starts a fraction away from the base of the first line. Take the needle into the fabric slightly under the ridge of the first line, coming up to catch the loop a little way along from where you started, creating a blanket stitch that lies between those of the first line and allowing the ridge to form on the opposite side.

Blanket stitch – striped

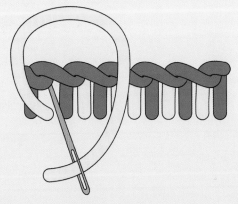

Work a line of blanket stitch (see page 27) leaving a small space between the stitches. When you have completed the row, work straight stitches between the blanket stitches. Start at the base and bury the needle under the ridge of the blanket stitch so that the end of each straight stitch is hidden.

Breton stitch – single

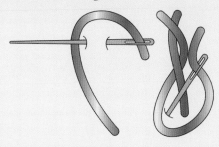

Form the right-hand stitch first. Bring your needle up at the top and make a straight stitch, going in at the bottom. Come up again at the top, close and slightly to the left of the first stitch. Moving down, whip the first stitch a couple of times and take the needle in at the bottom, slightly to the left of the first stitch.

Bullion knot

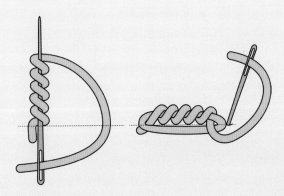

Come out of the fabric at the start of the space you wish to fill and go in again at the end of that space. Come out again at the start of the space. Leave a loop of thread on the top and don't pull the needle all the way through the fabric. Twist the thread around the needle as many times as you require. Holding the twists with the thumb and forefinger of your left hand, pull the needle through. Pull the working thread until the knot lies flat and take the needle back into the fabric at the start of the space. To make a looped bullion knot, wrap the thread more times than you need to fill the space available, so that the bullion knot will not lie completely flat but will loop up slightly.

Bullion lazy daisy stitch – double

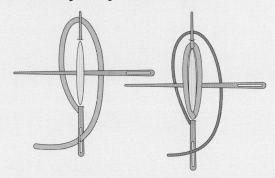

Work a bullion knot of the required length (see page 28). Insert a spare needle under the bullion knot as indicated in the diagram above. Bring the working needle up through the fabric just below the base of the bullion knot. Go back into the same hole coming up just about at the tip of the bullion knot. Guiding the thread under both sides of the spare needle and under the tip of the working needle, pull through. When you tighten the lazy daisy stitch try to ensure that it lies slightly underneath the bullion knot. This will cause the knot to pop out a bit, making it more pronounced. Finish the lazy daisy stitch with a small couching stitch that catches the loop, holding it in place. Work a second lazy daisy stitch around the first one in the same way, tightening it to lie slightly under the first lazy daisy stitch.

Buttonhole circle

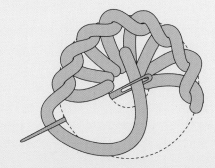

Come up on the outside circle. Take the needle down on the inside circle, and out again on the outside circle, with the loop of thread under the needle. Pull through and repeat, keeping the stitches close on the inner circle and further apart on the outside. When you meet up with where you started, complete the circle by catching the last buttonhole stitch with a couching stitch and going down where the first buttonhole stitch started.

Buttonhole – detached

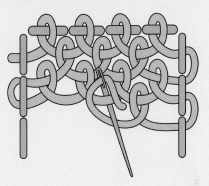

Surround the area that you intend to fill with small backstitches that you will use to anchor the detached buttonhole stitch. Bring your needle up on the side, from under the backstitch on the side, go over and under the first horizontal backstitch and making sure that the working thread is under the needle, pull through to form a buttonhole stitch. Go into the fabric, pushing in under the backstitch level with the ridge of the buttonhole stitch and come up from under the backstitch to start the next row.

Buttonhole flower

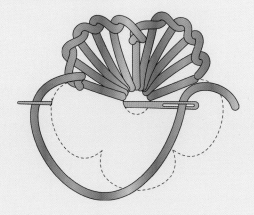

Come up on the outside in one of the valleys of the outline of the flower. Take the needle down on the inside circle, and out again on the outside line, coming out of the same hole as the straight stitch you have just made. Take the needle down on the inside circle, and out again on the outside line, with the loop of thread under the needle. Pull through and repeat, keeping the stitches close on the inner circle and further apart on the outside line. When you reach the bottom point of the next valley, work a small couching stitch over the buttonhole stitch you have just done. Come up again inside the buttonhole stitch in the same hole as the beginning of the couching stitch and continue working the buttonhole stitches that form the next petal. Work the small couching stitch at the bottom of each valley as this helps to define each petal. When you meet up with where you started, complete the circle by catching the last buttonhole stitch with a couching stitch and going down where the first straight stitch started.

Buttonhole foxglove stem

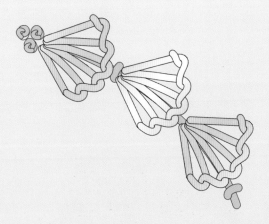

Start by working a stem, as depicted in green above, with a long straight stitch couched into a curve. With the same thread, work three to five French knots in a bunch at the tip of the stem. Thereafter, as depicted in pink above and start-ing with a straight stitch on the left, work groups of five buttonhole stitches in a fan shape, finishing each group with a couching stitch on the right. Start just below the French knots at the tip, working down the stem and making as many buttonhole bud groups as you need to cover most of the couched stem.

Buttonhole – long and short

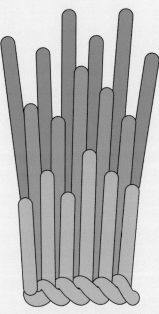

Use thread in three shades. Start with a single strand of the lightest thread by working close buttonhole stitch on the outside edge of the space you wish to fill, with the purl edge creating the outline of the shape. The straight, upward facing parts of the buttonhole stitches should be of differing, random lengths - as you would do for conventional long and short stitch shading. Working with thread that is a shade darker and starting slightly above the lightest colour, work straight stitches of random lengths tucking the ends between the straight parts of the buttonhole stitches. A third row would be done in a thread that is a shade darker. These stitches should also be of random lengths, making them alternately long and short on both ends unless they form the top row, in which case you will follow the outline of the shape.

Buttonhole stitch – layered

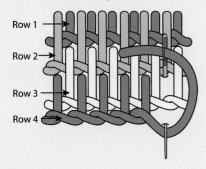

Row 1
Row 2
Row 3
Row 4

Referring to the diagram above, work you first line of buttonhole stitch as normal (dark purple). Start the next row, depicted as medium purple, slightly below the ridge of the first row. Go into the fabric at the same level that you went into the fabric when stitching the first row, coming up the bottom of the new row with the thread looped under the needle and pulling through. For the third (light purple) and subsequent rows start the row slightly below the ridge of the previous row. Go into the fabric immediately below the ridge of the first row with the thread looped under the needle and pulling through. Repeat as required. When you have covered the area you need to cover do one final row immediately adjacent to the row you have just done. The ridge of the stitch should lie against the ridge of the stitches in the previous row thereby filling in the gaps and outlining the edge at the same time. You will typically do this final row in the darkest colour.

Buttonhole stitch – up and down

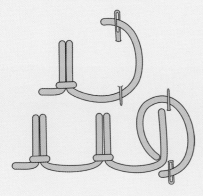

Working from left to right, bring the needle up on the bottom edge where you require the ridge. Take the needle in at the top edge, and out again at the bottom edge, with the thread looped under the needle. Pull through. Go over the thread, insert the needle on the line, bringing it up again adjacent to the upper part of the stitch, as depicted. Making sure that the thread is looped under the needle, pull upwards and then downwards to continue.

Buttonhole stitch – up and down, double

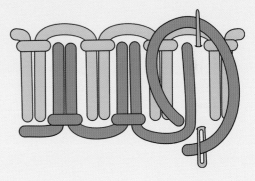

Following the instructions for up and down buttonhole stitch (above), work a row leaving enough space between each pair of stitches to accommodate another double stitch. Turning your work over, work a row of up and down buttonhole stitch, the upward facing parts of which are placed in the spaces left when you worked the first row, burying the ends of the upward facing parts under the ridge created in the previous row.

Buttonhole stitch – up and down, striped

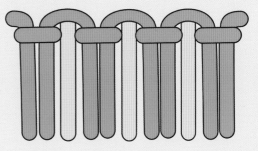

Following the instructions for up and down buttonhole stitch (see page 31), work a row leaving enough space between each pair of stitches to accommodate a straight stitch. With a contrasting colour, work straight stitches in the spaces working from the bottom and burying the end of the stitch under the ridge created by the up and down buttonhole stitch.

Cast-on buttonhole bar

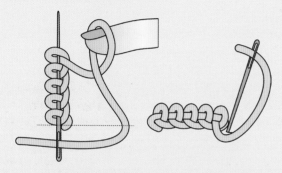

Bring the needle up at the beginning of the line. Take it in at the end of the line and bring it up again at the beginning of the line, making sure you don't snag the thread and leaving a loop of thread on the top. The needle should remain in the fabric, facing up. Twist the thread of the loop over your finger once and place it over needle, pull it to tighten down the needle. Cast on as many loops as you need to, pull the needle through, tighten the remaining thread of the original loop and go back into the fabric at the end of the line.

Chain stitch

Bring the needle up on the line and pull through. Take the needle back into the same hole and come up again where you want the chain stitch to end, loop the thread under the needle and pull

through. Staying inside the loop, go back into the same hole, loop the thread under the needle and pull through. Repeat as required and catch the last loop with a small couching stitch.

Chain stitch/Backstitch combination

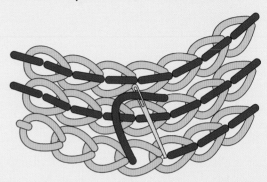

Work a row of chain stitch using shade no. 1. Thereafter, using shade no. 2, work a backstitch from the middle of the first chain stitch to the space just before the start of the chain stitch. Follow that with backstitches that start in the middle of the next chain stitch and go into the start of the backstitch in the previous chain stitch. Continue doing backstitch in this way, finishing up on the outside of the last chain stitch. When you do multiple rows of this stitch combination, it is sensible to complete the back stitch in the row before moving on to the next row of chain stitch because it is difficult to see where you should stitch if you have done all of the chain stitch before you start on the backstitch.

Chain stitch – interlaced, basic

Referring to the blue lines in the diagram, work a line of either traditional chain stitch (see page 32), or reverse chain stitch (see page 35). Thereafter, referring to the green lines and starting on the left, come up at the beginning, go under one side of the second chain stitch. Working backwards, go under the same side of the first chain stitch, go over the working thread and go under the one side of the third chain stitch. Working backwards, go under the same side of the second chain stitch, go over the working thread and go under the one side of the fourth chain stitch. Keep going in this way to the other end. When you have laced the penultimate stitch, go into the fabric below the last chain stitch. Catch the thread in the voile backing and come up again in the same place. Working backwards, go under the side of the last chain stitch, go over the working thread and go into the fabric below the last chain stitch. Interlace the other side in the same way.

Chain stitch – interlaced, double

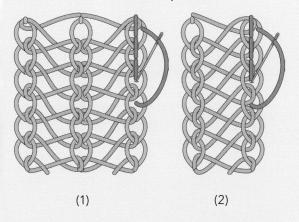

(1)   (2)

This version (1) is particularly suited to feathers.

As depicted by the green lines in the above diagram, starting from the base of the shape, work chain stitch up the middle and also on both sides of the shape trying to make sure that you have the same number of chain stitches in each row and that they are approximately opposite one another.

As you get towards the tip, make shorter stitches in the middle line and longer stitches on the side lines as they curve around the tip, finishing all three lines in the middle of the tip.

Following the pink lines, come up at the beginning of the middle row of chain stitch. Go under the top side of the chain stitch on one side and then go under the small couching stitch that holds that chain stitch in place.

#Crossing over, go under the top end of the second middle chain. Go under the bottom end of the first chain stitch in the middle row.

Crossing over, go under the top end of the second chain stitch on the side, then under the bottom end of the first chain stitch on the same side.#

Repeat from # to #, dropping a chain stitch on each side until you get to the end, curving around the tip and finishing where the two lines of chain stitch meet in the middle.

Interlace the other side in the same way.

With a contrasting thread work backstitch inside the chain stitches. Come up in the centre of the first side chain stitch at the base of the shape. Go in just outside the chain stitch at the base. Come up in the centre of the second chain stitch and go in in the centre of the first chain stitch. Keep going in this way until you get to the base on the other side, finishing on the outside of the final chain stitch. In the middle of the tip you should be able to seamlessly continue from the one row of side stitches to the other side row.

A simple version of this technique requires lines of chain stitch on either side of the space that are interlaced as depicted in diagram (2).

Chain stitch – interlaced, variation 1

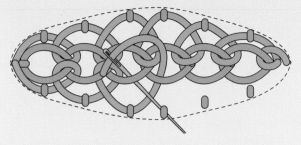

Referring to the green lines in the above diagram, work a horizontal line of either chain stitch (see page 32) or reverse chain stitch (see page 35). Using either the same or a contrasting thread, work vertical straight stitches on either side and approximately opposite the middle of each chain stitch, following the shape of the area you want to fill. Thereafter, following the blue lines, come up at the beginning and go through the first side straight stitch and go under one side of the second chain stitch. Working backwards, go under the same side of the first chain stitch, go over the working thread and go under the second side straight stitch. Go under one side of the third chain stitch. Working backwards, go under the same side of the second chain stitch, over the working thread and under the third side straight stitch. Keep going in this way to the other end. When you have laced the penultimate stitch, go through the last straight stitch and into the fabric below the last chain stitch. Catch the thread in the voile backing and come up again in the same place. Working backwards, go under the side of the last chain stitch, go over the working thread and go into the fabric below the last chain stitch. Interlace the other side in the same way.

Chain stitch – interlaced, variation 2

Referring to the pink lines in the above diagram,

work a horizontal line of either chain stitch (see page 32), or reverse chain stitch (see page 35). Using either the same or a contrasting thread, work vertical straight stitches above and approximately opposite the middle of each chain stitch, following the shape of the area you want to fill. Thereafter, following the top green lines, come up at the beginning and go through the first side straight stitch and go under one side of the second chain stitch. Working backwards, go under the same side of the first chain stitch, go over the working thread and go under the second side straight stitch. Go under one side of the third chain stitch. Working backwards, go under the same side of the second chain stitch, over the working thread and under the third side straight stitch. Keep going in this way to the other end. To interlace the bottom of the chain stitch and following the bottom green lines, come up at the beginning, go under one side of the second chain stitch. Working backwards, go under the same side of the first chain stitch, go over the working thread and go under the one side of the third chain stitch. Working backwards, go under the same side of the second chain stitch, go over the working thread and go under the one side of the fourth chain stitch. Keep going in this way to the other end.

Chain stitch – interlaced, variation 3

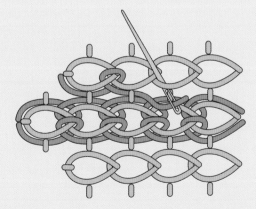

Referring to the pink lines in the above diagram, work a horizontal line of chain stitch (see page 32) or reverse chain stitch (see page 35). Using either the same or a contrasting thread, work vertical straight stitches on either side and approximately opposite the middle of each chain stitch. Work a second row of chain stitches that are close to the straight stitches on the side of the first row. Work vertical straight stitches on the far side of the chain stitches. Keep adding rows in this way until you have filled the shape. Thereafter, following the red lines, come up at the beginning of the first row and go through the first side straight stitch and go under one side of the second chain stitch. Working backwards, go under the same side of the first chain stitch, go over the working thread and go under the second side straight stitch. Go under one side of the third chain stitch. Working backwards, go under the same side of the second chain stitch, over the working thread and under the third side straight stitch. Keep going in this way to the other end. When you have laced the penultimate stitch, go through the last straight stitch and into the fabric below the last chain stitch. Catch the thread in the voile backing and come up again in the same place. Working backwards, go under the side of the last chain stitch, go over the working thread and go into the fabric below the last chain stitch. Interlace the other side in the same way.

Moving to the next row of chain stitch, work the interlacing in the same way as above but going through a shared straight stitch on the side that is adjacent to a previous row.

Chain stitch – reverse

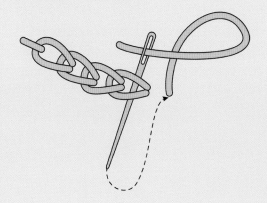

Working chain stitch in reverse gives a neater, more controlled result than you will achieve when working it the traditional way. Start with a short straight stitch. Come up on the line slightly further down. Take your needle under the backstitch and go back into same hole. Continue by coming up on the line slightly further down. Take your needle under both threads of the previous loop and go back into the same hole. Continue in this way finishing off by just going back into the same hole for the last loop.

Chain stitch – whipped

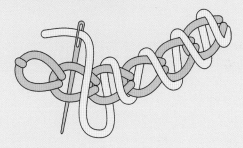

To whip chain stitch, bring your needle up adjacent to the beginning of the line of stitching. Take your needle and thread over, then under each stitch. It is advisable to use a tapestry needle when whipping. Using a contrasting colour thread is often effective.

Chain stitch – whipped, variation

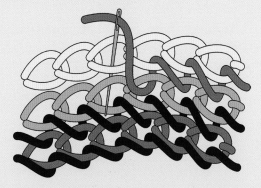

Work a single line of chain stitch. With a separate whipping thread on a tapestry needle, whip up the side of the chain stitch taking in only the outer (bottom) side of the loop. Work a second row of chain stitch next to the first, making sure that the stitches start and end level with the stitches in the first row of chain stitch. Whip the top side of the loop of the first row and the bottom side of the loop of the second row of chain stitch together with the whipping thread. Continue adding rows of chain stitch in this way, whipping before you start the next row. Whip the top side of the last row of chain stitch to complete.

Couching

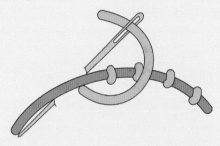

Use two threaded needles. Bring the first one up at the beginning of the line and lay it down. Catch it down with small stitches placed at intervals along the line. These small stitches should not have a tight tension.

Daisy trellis: see Trellis couching – daisy filling (page 47)

Detached buttonhole: see Buttonhole – detached (page 29)

Detached chain (lazy daisy) stitch

Bring the needle up on the line and pull through. Take the needle back into the same hole and come up again where you want the stitch to end, loop the thread under the needle and pull through. Catch the loop with a small couching stitch.

Detached chain stitch – double

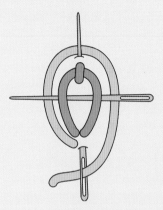

Use two shades of thread. Work the smaller detached chain using the darker thread. Place a tapestry needle under the two sides of the main part of the stitch as indicated in the diagram. Using the lighter thread, come up below the first detached chain. Take the needle back into the same hole and manipulate it so that it comes out where you will want to catch the loop with the small couching stitch. Make the threads of the loop lie under both sides of the horizontal needle and also the needle that will catch it. Tighten the stitch, work the small couching stitch to catch the loop and remove the horizontal needle, making sure that the inner detached chain remains slightly raised in the middle.

Double blanket stitch: see Blanket stitch – double (page 29)

Eye-stitch variation

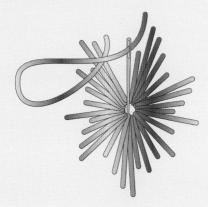

Come up on the outside and working in a clockwise direction, make straight stitches of varying lengths into the same hole in the middle. Pull reasonably tight so that the hole in the middle becomes a proper, visible hole that creates the 'eye'.

Feather stitch – closed

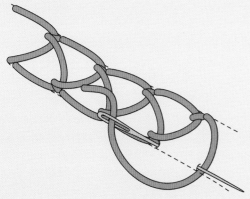

Come up on the bottom dotted line and go in on the top dotted line, leaving a loop of thread. Come up again below where you went in on the top dotted line and pick up the loop. Work a small couching stitch over the thread. You would not normally do this couching stitch when working feather stitch but because you are working on a curve it is best to secure the feather stitch so that it does not pull towards the centre. Come up again on the top line where you came out to work the couching stitch, go in on the bottom line, just below where you exited for the first stitch, leaving a loop. Come up further down the bottom line and

pick up the loop, securing it with a small couching stitch, coming up again where you came out to work the couching stitch. Keep going in this way.

Fly stitch

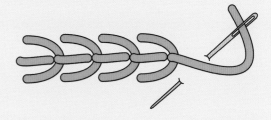

Start at the tip of your shape with a straight stitch. Come up on the left of that stitch, go in at the same level on the right, leaving a loop. Come up in the bottom hole of the straight stitch. Catch the loop and pull through. Make a straight stitch.

Fly stitch – variation

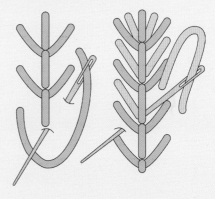

Start at the tip of your shape with a straight stitch. Come up on the left of that stitch, go in at the same level on the right, leaving a loop. Come up in the bottom hole of the straight stitch. Catch the loop and pull through. Make a straight stitch. Keep going in this way with a gap after each fly stitch and finish the line with a straight stitch. Thread up with a different colour thread. Work straight stitches between the fly stitches coming up on the outside in each gap and burying the end of each stitch under the ridge of the fly stitch.

FREESTYLE STITCHING

Where freestyle stitching has been used in the designs in this book, the stitches used are noted in the instructions. Note that the shape of the areas filled with specific stitches should be irregular, no squares or circles, and that other than at the edges, the areas filled should not line up with any other areas that have been filled with different stitches. Intersperse your stitching with single-wrap French knots to soften the effect and, also, to fill up spaces that can't be filled with the recommended stitches. You are aiming to create an overall texture. All the stitches used in freestyle stitching are listed alphabetically in this gallery from page 28 to 45.

French knot

Bring the needle up through the fabric, twist the thread over the needle once or twice and tighten. Go back into the fabric just next to where you came out. Pull the twists that are around the needle down to the bottom. Hold the thread and pull the needle through to form the knot.

French knot – extended (pistil stitch)

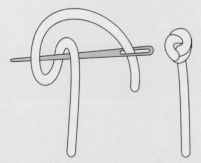

Bring the needle up through the fabric, twist the thread over the needle once or twice and tighten. Go back into the fabric away from where you came out. Pull the twists that are around the needle down to the bottom of the needle. Hold the thread and pull the needle through to form the knot.

French knot – loose

Bring the needle up through the fabric, loosely twist the thread over the needle two or three times. Tighten only slightly and go back into the fabric just next to where you came out. Pull the needle through controlling the twists as you do so, the aim being to achieve two or three loose loops of thread held down by the thread that goes into the fabric. Working a bunch of these together to fill an area creates the impression of foliage or flowers seen in the distance.

Heavy chain stitch

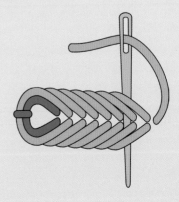

Make a small backstitch at the beginning of the line. Bring the needle up below the backstitch, go under the backstitch and back into where you came out to create a loop. Bring the needle up below the loop you have just made and make another loop through the backstitch. Bring the needle up below the loop you have just made and make a loop through the first loop. Continue by bringing the needle up below the loop just done and making a loop through the second last loop you made.

Herringbone stitch – interlaced

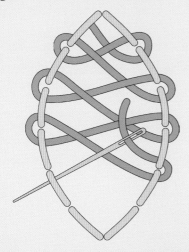

Work a foundation of backstitch on the lines of the shape. Come up under the first backstitch on the left-hand side, go under the second backstitch on the right-hand side. Snake round to go under the first backstitch on the right-hand side and go under the second backstitch on the left-hand side. Snake round to go under the first backstitch on the left-hand side and go under the third backstitch on the right-hand side. Keep going in this way until you have filled the shape, going into the fabric under the last backstitch at the bottom.

Herringbone stitch – raised

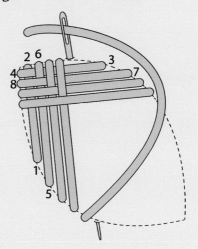

Bring your needle up at 1. Take it back in again at 2. Come up at 3 and go down at 4. Bring it up again at 5 and go into the fabric at 6. Keep going in this way until your shape has been filled. A subtle ridge will form in the centre of the shape.

Interlaced backstitch: see Backstitch – interlaced (page 26)

Interlaced chain stitch (all variations): see Chain stitch – interlaced (page 32)

Interlaced herringbone: see Herringbone stitch – interlaced (page 39)

Knotted cable-chain stitch

Working from top to bottom, bring your needle up at the beginning of the line. Make a small stitch under the line, take the working thread over and then under the needle. Pull through, first backwards and then forwards, to tighten the small knot. Pass the needle under the thread before the knot, go into the fabric on the right of the knot and bring your needle up on the line, making sure your thread is under the needle. Pull through to form a loop. Form the next knot by making a small stitch outside the loop and continuing as described.

Layered buttonhole: see Buttonhole stitch – layered (page 31)

Lazy daisy bud – three-petal

Referring to the instructions for detached chain (lazy daisy) stitch (see page 36), work three stitches in a trefoil shape. Work a French or colonial knot in the centre and at the base of the chain stitches. This can be made into a sweet flower by couching a stem going down from the base of the French or collonial knot.

Lazy daisy flower – nine-petal

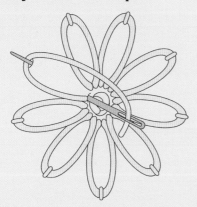

Referring to the instructions for detached chain stitch (see page 36), work nine stitches in a circle. Work a French or colonial knot in the centre and at the base of the chain stitches. You can increase or decrease the number of detached chain stitches in the circle.

Lazy daisy strawberry

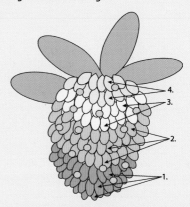

Starting at the base of the fruit, work the first short curved row along the bottom line with detached chain or lazy daisy stitches. Thereafter, work a longer curved row, with each subsequent row getting longer at the beginning and the end, and then getting shorter towards the top of the fruit. As you work each row, the bottom end of the detached chain stitches lay over the start of all the stitches in the row before. Referring to the rows marked 1 in the illustration above, work about three curved rows of detached chain stitches using the darkest pink thread. The three rows marked 2 are worked in a lighter shade of pink. The two rows marked 3 are worked with a light shade of yellow, finishing off with the two rows marked 4 which are worked in a darker shade of yellow. Finish off the fruit by working French knots evenly spaced here and there, placing them between the detached chain stitches in an even darker shade of yellow. The leaves that come out of the top are satin stitch leaves (see page 44).

Long and short buttonhole: see Buttonhole – long and short (page 30)

Long and short stitch shading

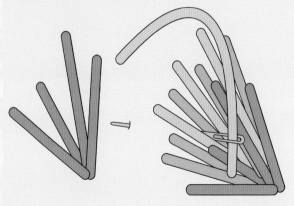

Work with a single strand of thread. Starting in the middle of the shape working first to the right and then returning to the middle and working to the left, stitch the darkest colour at the base first. Work straight stitches of random lengths from top to bottom fanning the stitches so that they favour the centre. Change to the medium colour thread for the next row, which is started slightly above the darkest colour. Work the stitches going into the fabric between the threads in the previous row. These stitches should also be of random lengths, making them alternately long and short on both ends. Change to the lightest colour for the top row. Following the top outline of the shape, work the third row going into the fabric between the threads in the previous row. These stitches should also be of random lengths, with the ragged edge at the bottom of the row.

Loop stitch

Come up in the middle of the line that you wish to cover. Go in at the top. Come up directly below, on the bottom line, go under the first stitch and over the loop of thread and pull through. Go in at the top. Come up at the bottom and go under the second stitch, over the loop of thread and pull through. Repeat as required. If the rib that is created is not sitting where you would like it to be, it can be moved by adjusting the tension of the stitches.

Loop, weaving and pistil stitch combination

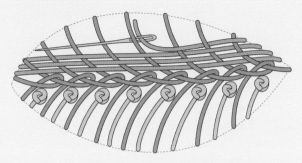

If this combination is used to fill a feather, start by working loop stitch (see above) from the base to the tip of the feather. Thereafter, using two strands of cotton as specified for the project, weave over and under the side, long stitches of the loop stitch on one side of the feather, alternating the sequence in each row so that where you have gone over a thread in one row you will go under it in the next row. Working on the other side of the feather, do pistil stitches (extended French knots, see page 38) starting on the outside edge of the feather, finishing with the knot adjacent to the loops in the middle.

Meandered running stitch

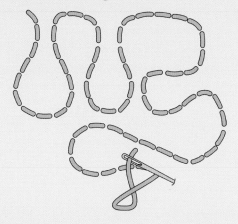

Used by quilters and usually done free hand on a sewing machine, hand-stitched meandering involves working running stitch in swirls and paths that do not cross over each other. Because the fabric is stretched tightly in a frame, you cannot take the needle in and out of the sandwiched layers in one action. Rather take the needle down, pull through, then return to the top by taking the needle up in a separate action. Keep your tension tight so that the sandwiched layers are pulled together.

Outline stitch

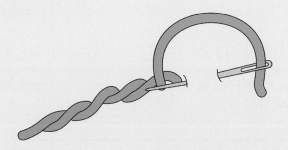

It is usually best to do this stitch with one strand of thread. Working from left to right, come up at the beginning of the line. Go in on the line and before pulling the thread through, come up halfway back on the line. Pull through. Go into the fabric halfway further and come up just a little past halfway back, so that you are not coming up in the same hole as where the first stitch finished. Continue to the end of the outline.

Ox-head stitch

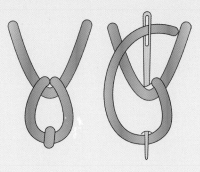

Also called tête de boeuf or bull's-head stitch. Bring your needle up on the left, take it down on the right and before pulling through, come up in the centre a little way below and catch the loop as you would for fly stitch. Pull through. Take your needle back into the same hole and before pulling through, come up below the previous stitch and catch the loop as you would for a detached chain or lazy daisy. Finish with a small couching stitch to catch the loop.

Pistil stitch: see French knot – extended (page 38)

Raised chain stitch

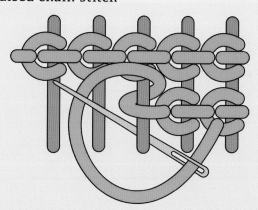

Work a ladder of straight stitch over the area. Come up at the beginning of the ladder in the centre of the first bar. Go over and weave under the bar to the left. Bring the thread around the front and to the right, go under the bar and over the thread. Pull through to form a small knot.

Raised chain stitch – woven

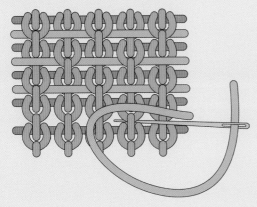

Fill the area with raised chain stitch (see page 42). With a contrasting thread on a tapestry needle, weave over and under the threads that run between the raised chain knots, alternating the sequence in each row so that where you have gone over a thread in one row, you will go under it in the next row. Take your needle into the fabric at the end of each row, coming up at the beginning for the next row.

Raised herringbone: see Herringbone stitch – raised (page 39)

Reverse chain stitch: see Chain stitch – reverse (page 35)

Rhodes stitch

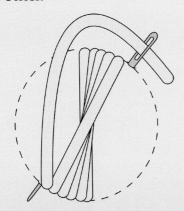

Divide the circle equally by bisecting it with a straight stitch worked from top to bottom. Come up at the top, slightly to the left of the last stitch and go in the bottom, crossing over and going in

slightly to the right of the previous stitch. Repeat until you have filled the circle.

Running stitch

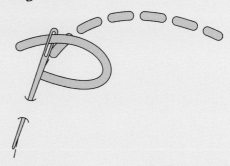

Stitch a continuous line by passing the needle over and under the fabric making sure that the stitches and the gaps in between are of equal length. Usually the gaps are half the length of the stitches.

Satin stitch

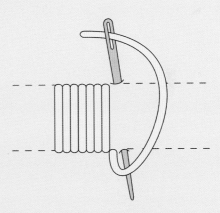

Working from left to right, bring your needle up at the bottom and in at the top, and come out at the bottom again. Place your stitches close together so that no fabric is showing. It is best to work over the shortest side and stitches can also be placed diagonally.

Satin-stitch leaf

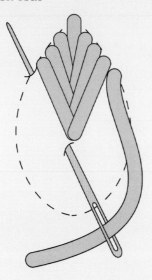

Starting at the top of the leaf, come out at the tip and do a straight stitch to where the vein of the leaf starts. Thereafter, work a straight stitch on each side. Each pair goes into the same hole at the bottom. Drop down low in the centre to keep a sharp stitching angle.

Sheaf stitch

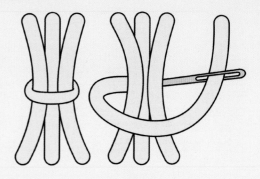

Working three vertical straight stitches, start with the middle stitch. Place a straight stitch to the right of that stitch. Do a stitch to the left of the middle stitch, but before you tighten it, bring your needle up adjacent to the centre of the middle stitch. Pull through, tightening the left-hand straight stitch. Do a straight stitch over the middle of the three stitches, tucking it under the right-hand stitch, going in adjacent to the middle stitch to pull the three stitches together. You can do a second stitch over the middle if you wish.

Seeding

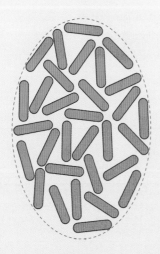

Fill the space with small, straight stitches. All the stitches should be done at random and should be of equal length as depicted in the diagram.

Single-weaving shading

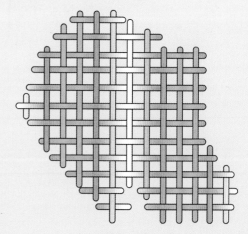

Working with a single strand of stranded cotton, create the warp stitches from top to bottom making them between 1 and 2 mm apart. Work the weft stitches the same distance apart, alternating the sequence in each row so that where you have gone over a thread in one row, you will go under it in the next row. Depending on the shape you are filling, you may need to create breaks in the stitches as indicated in the diagram. If you would like to create a shaded effect, work some warp and weft stitches in a darker or lighter colour.

Single weaving with stranded cotton

Working with two strands of thread, create a ladder – or warp – with straight stitches usually over the shortest side of the shape. Thereafter, working at right angles to the straight stitches, moving from side to side and back again, weave over and under the straight stitches. When you have gone over and under in one row, go under and over in the next row. Pack the weaving – or weft – rows closely together to create an interesting textured finish.

Split backstitch: see Backstitch – split (page 26)

Stem stitch

Working from left to right, come up just above the line, go in just below the line and come up halfway back, just above the line. Pull through. When using stem stitch as an outline stitch, come up on the line and go in on the line.

Stem stitch – raised

Working from right to left, create a straight stitch ladder which forms the basis of this technique. Working from left to right, bring your needle up slightly past the last straight stitch in the ladder. Go over and under the straight stitches in continuous lines, always starting from the same side, working in the same direction.

Striped blanket stitch: see Blanket stitch – striped (page 28)

Trellis couching — basic

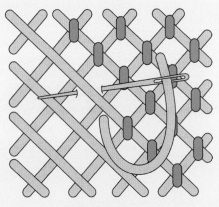

Work a layer of long straight stitches across the area. These can be vertical or diagonal. Work another layer of long straight stitches that are placed at right angles to the first layer. Work small, straight couching stitches over the intersection of the stitches.

Trellis couching — cross-stitch couching variation 1

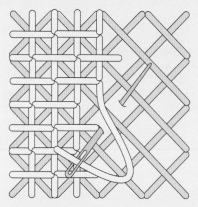

Work a layer of diagonal long straight stitches across the area. Work another layer of long straight stitches that are placed at right angles to the first layer. Working from the middle of the empty block, to the middle of the next empty block, work cross stitches over each intersection. All the cross stitches will go into, or come out of, the same hole in the middle of the empty block.

Trellis couching — cross-stitch couching variation 1 shaded

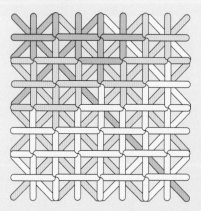

To give a shaded effect to trellis with cross-stitch couching, thread up with the colours you want to use on separate needles so that you have all of them available to use as you see fit. Referring to the diagram above and starting with the first layer, use the darkest colour in areas that would need to be darker, moving to the medium and lighter threads as you want an area to look lighter. Nec-

essarily, because the trellis stitches spread over a large area, there will be areas with mixed shades, but this doesn't matter provided the general trend is towards light or dark. When working the second layer, the cross stitches, continue this trend with some areas comprising only dark threads over both layers, others a mix of dark and medium, or medium and light, and others a mix of all three depending on the shape of the area and, also, how you would like the shading to be.

Trellis couching — cross-stitch couching variation 2

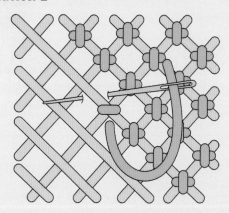

Work a layer of diagonal long straight stitches across the area. Work another layer of long straight stitches that are placed at right angles to the first layer. Work small cross stitches over the intersection of the stitches.

Trellis couching — cross-stitch filling

Using thread shade no. 1, work a layer of pairs of long straight stitches across the area. These can be horizontal or diagonal. Work another layer of pairs of long straight stitches that are placed at right angles to the first layer. Using thread shade no. 2, work small, straight couching stitches over each thread of the intersections. Work from the outside into the middle of each intersection, each stitch going into the same hole.

Trellis couching – daisy filling

Work a layer of long, diagonal straight stitches across the area. Work another layer of long straight stitches that are placed at right angles to the first layer. Work vertical, small, straight couching stitches over the intersection of the stitches. Work four detached chain stitches out from the couched intersection towards the middle of the empty block between the lines of the trellis. All of the steps in this stitch combination can be worked with the same thread, or you can vary the shades.

Trellis couching – triangular filling

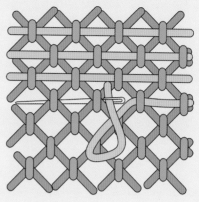

Using thread shade 1, work a layer of long, diagonal straight stitches across the area. Work another layer of long straight stitches that are placed at right angles to the first layer. Work vertical, small, straight couching stitches over the intersection of the stitches. These can be with the same thread, or another shade. Come through the fabric with a different shade on a tapestry needle. Go under each couching stitch making a long horizontal line, which goes into the fabric when you reach the other side.

Trellis couching – woven

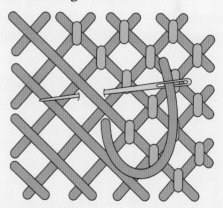

Using thread shade 1, work a layer of long straight stitches across the area. These can be horizontal or diagonal. Work another layer of long straight stitches that are placed at right angles to the first layer. Using thread shade 2, work small, straight couching stitches over the intersection of the long stitches.

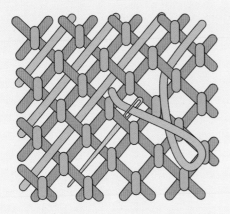

Using thread shade 3, weave over and under the shade 1 lines.

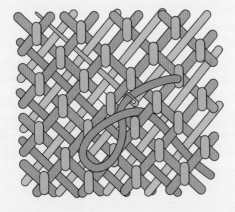

Using thread shade 4, and working at right angles, weave under the first of layer of trellis (shade 1 stitches) and over the weaving that you have just done (shade 3).

Up and down buttonhole stitch: see Buttonhole stitch – up and down (page 31)

Up and down buttonhole stitch, double: see Buttonhole stitch – up and down, double (page 31)

Up and down buttonhole stitch, striped: see Buttonhole stitch – up and down, striped (page 31)

Van Dyke stitch variation

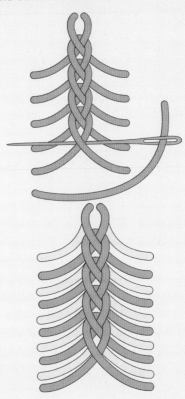

Bring the thread up on bottom left and going diagonally upwards, insert it centre right. Come up just next to where you went in on centre-left and go in again on bottom-right. Come up at bottom left, just below the first stitch. Going diagonally upwards, weave under the two stitches above the crossover point. Go in again on bottom right. Keep going in this way until you have filled the area. With a different thread, often contrasting, work straight stitches between the existing stitches. Come up on the side, go in in the centre burying the needle under the ridge created by the Van Dyke stitch. Do this on both sides.

Vermicelli couching

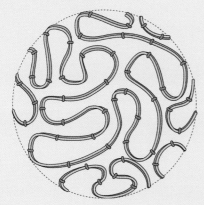

Thread a needle with two strands of thread and another with a single strand of thread. Come through the fabric with the two-strand needle and couch that thread into a series of rounded squiggles that move all over the area that you wish to cover, but never cross over each other. At the edges of the section go into the fabric and come up again further along continuing the pattern.

Vermicelli couching – two-tone variation

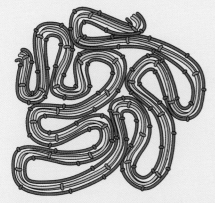

For a two-tone variation, follow the instructions for vermicelli couching (see above) working with two strands of cotton couched down with a single strand in the lighter of two shades. Make sure that the swirls are large enough to accommodate the second shade. The second shade requires a darker tone and is a single strand couched with a single strand, swirling between the existing couching on both sides of each line.

Wheatear stitch

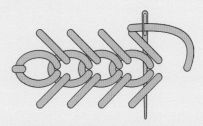

Working from left to right, work a detached chain, starting just below and stretching to the beginning. Place a diagonal straight stitch on each side of this stitch. Come up slightly below, work a loop through all the threads of the straight and detached chain stitches. Place a diagonal straight stitch on each side of this loop. Repeat as required.

Wheatear stitch variation

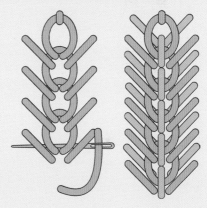

Work a line of wheatear stitch following the guidelines above. With a contrasting thread, work diagonal straight stitches between the side stitches of the wheatear stitch, burying the end of each stitch beneath the detached chain part of the wheatear stitch. With the same contrasting thread, work backstitch down the middle, coming up in the middle of the second detached chain stitch, going into the fabric in the middle of the top detached chain stitch. Come up in the middle of the third detached chain stitch, go into the same hole as you came out of in the second detached chain stitch. Keep going like this with the contrasting thread all the way down the line.

Whipped backstitch: see Backstitch – whipped (page 27)

Whipped chain stitch: see Chain stitch – whipped (page 35)

Whipped chain stitch variation: see Chain stitch – whipped variation (page 35)

Woven spider's web circle

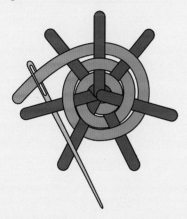

Work five to seven straight stitches, radiating out from a central point. Come up adjacent to the centre and weave a circle by going under one stitch then under the next. Repeat in a spiral until the stitches are covered and the circle is full.

Woven trellis couching: see Trellis couching – woven (page 47)

WORKING WITH TWISTED THREAD

The easiest way to convert stranded cotton into cord with which to embroider is to acquire a Spinster tool. It is, however, possible to twist it by turning it between your index finger and thumb, or to place a pencil in the loop and turn that.

- If you are twisting a double strand of thread cut a two-strand length of thread that measures approximately 1 m (1.1 yd) and tie an overhand knot on each end of the thread.
- Alternatively, for a twisted single strand, cut a 1 m (1.1 yd) length of thread, fold over a loop secured with an overhand knot on each end of the thread.
- Loop one end over something that won't move, like a cup-hook or a doorknob.
- Loop the other end over the hook on the Spinster and pull the yarn taut.
- Now wind the threads until they are firmly twisted together. If you don't have a spinster tool, pull the yarn taut and twist with your hands.
- Test from time to time by relaxing the tension and allowing the threads to twist around one another.
- When you are happy with the twist, double the twisted thread over by placing the two ends together.
- Hang the Spinster, or something heavy, at the fold to add weight so that it will twist together evenly.
- Pull all the threads off the cup hook or doorknob.
- Holding the ends together, allow the thread to hang from your fingers and twist freely.
- Once they stop twisting, do an overhand knot at the raw ends to keep them together. Snip off the raw ends after the knot for the sake of neatness.
- Thread the folded end onto a size 22 or 24 chenille needle and embroider with it as if it were normal thread.

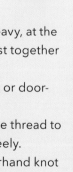

Bead-embroidery stitches

Attaching a bead with a bead

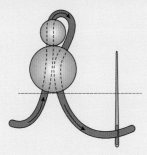

Bring your needle up through the fabric at the correct point. Pick up the larger and then the smaller bead. Return down through the larger bead and tighten the thread. The smaller bead holds the larger bead in place.

Attaching a single bead

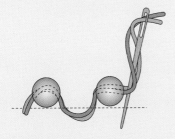

Bring your needle up through the fabric and pick up a bead. Pull the bead down the thread until it touches the fabric. Slide the needle down between the two threads until it touches the bead and go back into the fabric at that point. This will ensure that the length of the stitch holding the bead is correct and is a particularly useful way to attach bugle beads.

Bead circles

Bring the needle up through the fabric. Pick up as many beads as you require to make the size of circle that you need.

From the beginning of the line of beads, take the needle through the first three beads for a second time, making sure that you do not snag the thread with the needle. Go into the fabric, having left enough space to accommodate the three beads that have a double string of thread. Pull through, manipulating the beads so that they form a circle.

With the same thread, work a small couching stitch between the beads, over the circle of thread that holds the bead circle. If you pull that circle of thread out a little as you stitch, the bead circle will form more perfectly

Bead couching

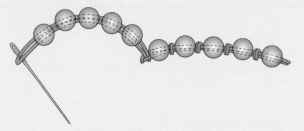

Pick up not less than two and not more than five beads. Lay them along the line that you need to follow, estimate about the width of a bead and go through the fabric. Push the beads to the beginning and couch over the thread between the beads, pulling the line into place as you go. Bring the needle up immediately after the last bead and pick up the next group of beads. Keep going in this way. When you reach the end of the line, go through the fabric, catch the thread in the voile backing fabric and return through the same hole. Run the thread through the whole line of beads, going into the fabric at the beginning and tugging the thread to tighten. This pulls the line of beads neatly into place.

Beaded backstitch

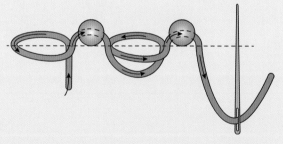

Start as you would for backstitch, a little way down the line. Go in at the beginning of the line. Come up in the hole where you started the backstitch. Pick up the bead; pull it down the thread until it touches the fabric. Slide the needle down between the two threads until it touches the bead and go back into the fabric at that point. Come up further along the line to start the next backstitch, going into the same hole that you went into when you attached the bead. Keep going in this way.

Beaded drizzle stitch

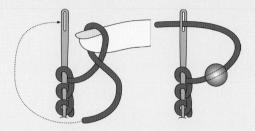

Come up through the fabric in the correct spot. Unthread the needle and put the needle into the fabric just next to where you came up. Place your index finger under the thread, rotate your finger to make a loop, which you then slip over the needle and tighten. Cast on as many of these loops as you need (three to ten). Thread the yarn onto a beading needle, pick up a bead, take the thread off the needle and rethread it into the needle onto which you did your cast-on stitches. Pull it through the fabric and come up to do the next one.

Beaded fly stitch with variation

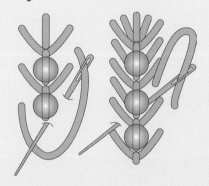

Start at the tip with a 4 mm (⅛") straight stitch. Come up on the left and go down on the right of the straight stitch, leaving a loop. Come up at the bottom of the straight stitch, catching the loop before you tighten. Pick up a bead and go into the fabric below it, leaving enough room for the bead to sit comfortably. Leaving a space of about 1 mm on the left side, start the next fly stitch. To vary this stitch, thread up with a different colour and work straight stitches between each pair of fly stitches, starting on the outside and burying the stitch under the ridge of the fly stitch.

Beaded knotted cable-chain stitch

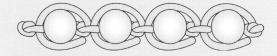

Work a line of knotted cable-chain stitch (see page 39). As you work, make sure that the loops are large enough to accommodate the bead you are intending to use in the space inside the loops (but not too large). When you have completed the line of stitching, thread a single strand of cotton onto a bead-embroidery needle, double it over and knot the two tails together. Come up as close as possible to the cable-chain knot at the start of the loop, pick up the bead and go back into the fabric as close as possible to the knot at the end of the loop.

Beaded wheatear stitch

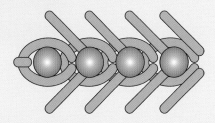

Working from top to bottom with a doubled-over single strand of thread and a needle that will go through a bead, work a detached chain, starting just below and stretching to the beginning of the shape. Place a diagonal straight stitch on each side of this stitch. Come up slightly below, work a loop through all the threads of the straight and detached chain stitches. Place a diagonal straight stitch on each side of this loop. Repeat as required until the shape is filled. Come up inside the loop created by the detached chain, slightly below the centre of the space, pick up a bead and go into the fabric allowing enough space for the bead to sit comfortably. Work your way up the line placing a bead in the centre of each detached chain stitch.

Beaded wheatear stitch with variation

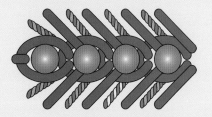

Work beaded wheatear stitch as explained before. With a contrasting thread work straight stitches from the side, between the side arms of the wheatear stitch, ending the stitch by tucking it under the detached chain stitch and going into the fabric.

Caged flat-back crystal

- Hold the flat-back crystal in place on the circle drawn for its placement.
- Use a waste thread that is a completely different colour from the thread you will use to stitch the cage that holds the flat-back crystal in place.
- Come through the fabric at the top of the crystal. Go into the fabric at the bottom, thus forming a straight stitch that goes down the midline of the crystal.
- Now work three more stitches to form a star that holds the crystal in place. The first should go over the horizontal midline. The last two go from top right to bottom left and then from top left to bottom right. When working the last two stitches, whip under the intersection of the first two stitches. This holds them all together and stops them from sliding off the crystal.
- Finish off by coming up one more time and doing a knot over the intersection. This will make it easy to pull these stitches out.

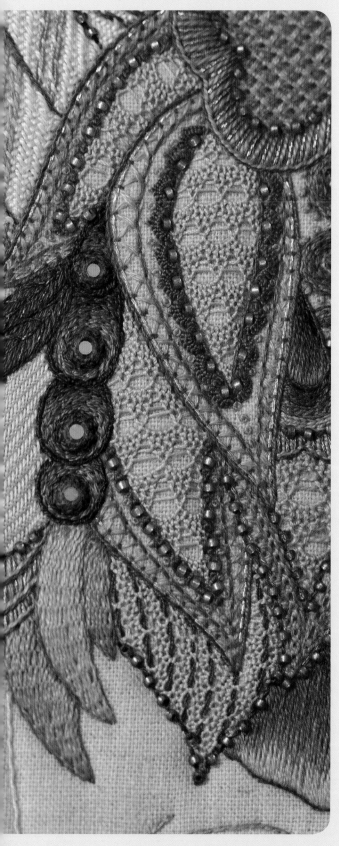

- Using a single strand of cotton, do a circle of back stitch around and adjacent to the crystal. A 34ss crystal would need about 12 backstitches whilst eight backstitches are about right for a 20ss crystal.

- Using the same thread, continue by working a detached buttonhole stitch under each backstitch.

- When you get back around to the first buttonhole stitch, take your needle through the loop of that stitch to secure the end of the row and continue in the opposite direction, working into each of the loops created in the first row.

- If you are attaching a 20ss crystal it only requires two rows of detached buttonhole stitch.

- If you are attaching a 34ss crystal, work a third row in the same way.

- When you reach the end of the final row of detached buttonhole stitch, continue in the same direction, whipping through each of the loops.

- When you get back to where you started the whipping stitches, pull the thread to tighten the last row and to make sure that it fits snugly against the crystal.

- Weave the needle through the detached buttonhole stitches and take it through the fabric to end off.

- Remove the waist-thread stitches that temporarily held the crystal in place.

Needle-lace techniques

GENERAL INSTRUCTIONS

Terms and abbreviations

- RL work right to left
- LR: work left to right
- BS: backstitch
- DBH: detached buttonhole stitch
- TB: tulle bar
- Step down: go into the fabric, burying the thread under the nearest backstitch that is level with the ridge of the detached buttonhole stitch. Come up from under the backstitch at the point where you need to start the next row

(Find the basic stitches in the embroidery stitch gallery from page 26.)

- All the stitches in this gallery are based on needle-lace techniques that have been modified for use as embroidery stitches.
- If you are new to needle-lace techniques, try the techniques on a scrap of fabric.
- It is almost impossible to create a smooth edge to your needle lace. Try to be as even and smooth as you can but be aware that you will need to either outline the area or modify the edge in some way.
- Always work with your fabric stretched taut in a hoop to prevent puckering.
- Use a size 7 or 8 embroidery needle to work the backstitches (BS) (see page 26) and a size 26 or 28 tapestry needle to work the detached buttonhole stitches (DBH) (see page 29).
- Each shape that you wish to fill with needle lace should be surrounded with BS. Use these stitches to both anchor the first lace row and to define the area.
- Don't expect your BS to be perfect. It's not

a perfect world. Use them as a guide and an anchor only. Adjust your tension and counting to suit the DBH, not the BS.

- The majority of needle-lace techniques use DBH.
- Each instruction notes the length of the BS in the top row.
- It usually doesn't matter which direction you choose to stitch your needle lace. You make life easier for yourself if you choose to work the first row on the edge that will give you the longest and straightest row, decreasing or increasing from there.
- Always make sure that the beginning and end of each row are approximately level with one another.
- When working further down, always make sure that you space your rows so that the sides of the needle lace are neither bunching up, nor stretching down too far. If you are unsure of where to come up at the beginning of a row, pull the middle section of the row you have just completed down with the point of your needle, see how far it stretches, then come up for the start of your row level with that point.

Working to the shape you need to fill

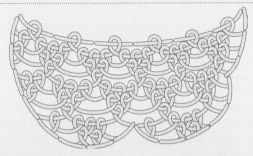

The above diagram is based on needle-lace stitch no. 9 which features in the pheasant project in this book (see page 135).

1. The first row has been worked on the longest line. This means that you won't need to increase, just decrease.

2. At the beginning and end of each row you are cognizant of the pattern you are working, adjusting it to accommodate the space you have available.

3. Note that in some instances, only one or two of the DBS needed in a group are worked into the loop in the previous row.

4. If you are in doubt as to whether you should work a stitch, it is better to put it there rather than leave it out as you could be in danger of being left with a gaping hole. You never want a hole, if you can avoid it.

Completing the needle-laced area

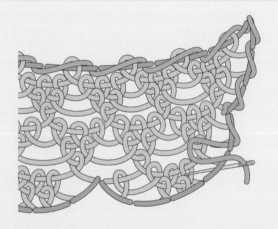

1. Because of the nature and size of the shapes that are filled in this book, go into the fabric at the end of each row, coming up through the fabric at the beginning of the next. This is called the step down.

2. When working the last row, come up from under the BS in line with where you need to be, work the detached buttonhole stitch and go back into the fabric, burying the needle under the BS at the bottom, encouraging the needle lace to stretch evenly down to the bottom.

3. This means that, other than anchoring the stitches in the top row, you will not work through the BS on the sides and bottom of the shape.

4. In some of the projects you will be instructed to work an outline on top of the backstitches in which case, follow those instructions.

5. If not, you may be advised to finish the needle-lace shape by whipping the backstitch with the same thread used to work the backstitches and the needle lace.

6. Work each portion of the backstitch separately, coming up in the same hole as the backstitch at the beginning and going back into the same hole at the end.

7. If necessary, catch the thread in the voile backing fabric before coming up to start the next whipping line.

THE PATTERNS

Stitch no. 2

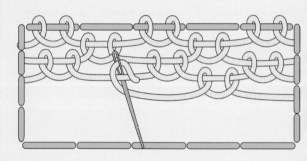

PREPARATION:
BS outline.

TOP ROW STITCH LENGTH:
To accommodate 2 x DBH.

1. Working LR, [2 x DBH into first BS, miss a BS]. Repeat [to] to end. Step down.
2. Working RL, 2 x DBH into each loop. Step down.

Keep working rows in this way until you have filled the required space. Following the instructions for the bottom row in the general tips, attach the detached buttonhole stitch at the bottom.

Stitch no. 9 with variation

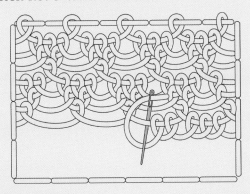

PREPARATION:
BS outline.

TOP ROW STITCH LENGTH:
To accommodate 3 x DBH.

1. Working RL, 1 x DBH into each BS. Step down.
2. #Working LR, 3 x DBH into each long loop between the single detached buttonhole stitches in the previous row. Step down.
3. Working RL, [1 x DBH into next loop, 1 x DBH into next loop, miss 1 loop]. Repeat [to] to end. Step down.
4. Working LR, [1 x DBH in small loop, miss large loop]. Repeat [to] to end. Step down.#

Keep working the rows from # to # until you have filled the required space. Following the instructions for the bottom row in the general tips, attach the detached buttonhole stitch at the bottom.

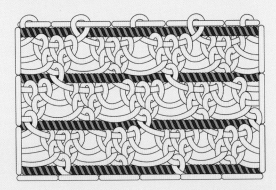

Referring to the project instructions to determine how many strands of thread you need to use and then to the instructions for working with twisted thread at the end of the embroidery gallery (see page 50), twist a length of cord. Thread the cord onto a 22 or 24 chenille needle and weave it over and under the single stitches in row 1 and thereafter in all the rows described as row 4 and shown in the previous diagram.

I have suggested weaving with a chenille needle because you would need a large tapestry needle to accommodate the twisted thread and it really is so difficult to get a large tapestry needle through the fabric. So, use a chenille needle and be careful not to snag the existing needle lace as you weave each row.

Stitch no. 10

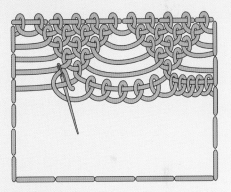

PREPARATION:
BS outline.

TOP ROW STITCH LENGTH:
To accommodate 2 x DBH.

1. Working LR, 2 x DBH into each BS. Step down.
2. #Working RL, [miss 1 loop, 1 x DBH into each of the next 4 loops]. Repeat [to] to end. Step down.
3. Working LR, [miss large loop, 1 x DBH into each of the next 3 loops]. Repeat [to] to end. Step down.
4. Working RL, [miss large loop, 1 x DBH into each of the next 2 loops]. Repeat [to] to end. Step down.
5. Working LR, [miss large loop, 1 x DBH into the small loop]. Repeat [to] to end. Step down.
6. Working RL, 5 x DBH into each large loop. Step down.#

Keep working the rows from # to # until you have filled the required space. Following the instructions for the bottom row in the general tips, attach the detached buttonhole stitch at the bottom.

Stitch 1 variation filler

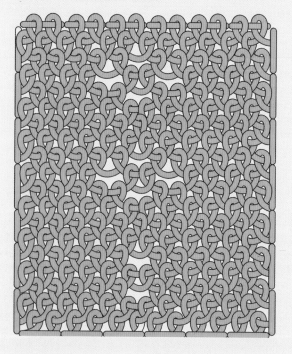

PREPARATION:
BS outline.

TOP ROW STITCH LENGTH:
To accommodate 2 x DBH.

1. Working LR, 2 x DBH into each backstitch. Step down.
2. #Working RL, 1 x DBH into each loop between the DBH in the previous row. Step down.
3. Work out approximately where the two middle stitches are in the previous row and working LR, 1 x DBH into each loop between the DBH in the previous row. When you reach the two middle stitches in the previous row, miss the gap between those two stitches and then continue to the end working 1 x DBH into each loop between the DBH in the previous row. Step down.

4. Working RL, 1 x DBH into each gap between the stitches in the previous row. When you get to the two stitches that lie before the large loop that you made in the previous row, miss the gap between them. Work 2 x DBH into the large loop, miss the gap between the next two stitches in the previous row and continue to the end working 1 x DBH into each loop between the DBH in the previous row. Step down.
5. Working LR, 1 x DBH into each loop between the DBH in the previous row. When you reach the large loop that you made in the previous row, work 2 x DBH into that loop. Miss the next gap – these are between the two stitches that you worked into the large loop. Work 2 x DBH into the next large loop and continue to the end working 1 x DBH into each loop between the DBH in the previous row. Step down.
6. Working RL, 1 x DBH into each loop between the DBH in the previous row. When you reach the large loop that you created in the previous row, work 2 x DBH into that loop and continue to the end working 1 x DBH into each loop between the DBH in the previous row. Step down.
7. Working LR, 1 x DBH into each loop between the DBH in the previous row. Step down.#
8. Repeat from # to # another two times to create three of the little diamond shaped 'flower' impressions.
9. Working RL, 1 x DBH into each loop between the DBH in the previous row. Step down.
10. [Working LR, 1 x DBH into each loop between the DBH in the previous row until you get to the middle. Miss one gap between the stitches in the previous row, directly below the previous middle gaps and continue to the end, working 1 x DBH into each loop between the DBH in the previous row. Step down.
11. Working RL, work 1 x DBH into each loop between the DBH in the previous row until you get to the middle. Work 2 x DBH into the large loop that you created in the previous row. Continue to the end, working 1 x DBH into each loop between the DBH in the previous row. Step down.]

12. Repeat from [to] until you get towards the tip of the area that you need to fill. You may find that you run out of space to create the holes in the pattern. If that happens, complete the area doing rows of 1 x DBH in each gap.

Secure the bottom of the lace by coming up from under the backstitch at the bottom, working a single DBH in the gap immediately above, and go back into the fabric under the backstitch line.

Claude filler no. 2

Claude filler no. 1

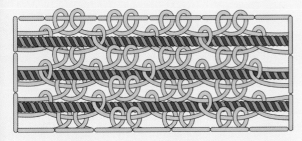

PREPARATION:
BS outline.

TOP ROW STITCH LENGTH:
To accommodate 2 x DBH.

1. Working LR, [2 x DBH into first BS, miss a BS]. Repeat [to] to end. Step down.
2. Working RL, 1 x DBH into each loop. Step down.
3. Keep working these two rows until you have filled the required space.
4. Join it to the BS at the bottom by working either one or two DBH stitches into the loops of the previous row, depending on what row you are doing when you get there. Come up from under the BS at the bottom, work the DBH stitch(es) and go back into the fabric under the BS, thereafter moving on to the next place you need to come up.
5. With a strand of metallic thread as noted in the instructions of the project, weave over and under the single DBH stitches worked in each and every row 2.

PREPARATION:
BS outline.

TOP ROW STITCH LENGTH:
To accommodate 2 x DBH.

1. Working LR, [2 x DBH into first BS, miss a BS]. Repeat [to] to end. Step down.
2. Working RL, 1 x DBH into each loop. Step down.
3. Repeat rows 1 and 2 three times so that you have four sets. When you do the final row step down, come up 4 mm (⅛") below where you finished the previous row.
4. Changing direction, work 2 x DBH into the first loop of the previous row.
5. Turning your work sideways, work 4 x DBH into the loop that led up to the first of the 2 x DBH.
6. Repeat to the end of the row and step down. This is the row into which you will weave silk ribbon, called the insertion row.
7. Changing direction, work 2 x DBH into each loop between the buttonhole bars. This is equivalent to row 1 above. Step down.

8. Repeat steps 2 to 6, continuing in this way until you have filled the space. As you work down the shape you will find that you might want to put in an insertion row before the shape narrows too much to accommodate one. In that case do less of the sets in rows 1 and 2, adding the insertion row sooner.

9. Join it to the backstitch at the bottom by working either one or two DBH stitches into the loops of the previous row, depending on what row you are doing when you get there. Come up from under the BS at the bottom, work the DBH stitch(es) and go back into the fabric under the BS and thereafter, moving on to the next place you need to come up.

10. With a strand of metallic thread as noted in the instructions of the project, weave over and under the single DBH stitches worked in each and every row 2.

11. Thread 2 mm silk ribbon, as noted in the instructions of the project, onto a size 24 or 26 tapestry needle and weave over and under the buttonhole bars that you made in steps 4 and 5.

Colin filler no. 1

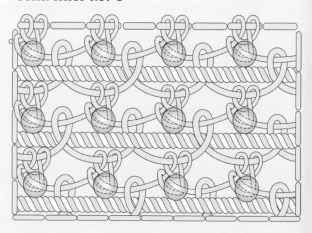

PREPARATION:
BS outline.

TOP ROW STITCH LENGTH:
To accommodate 2 x DBH.

1. Working LR, [2 x DBH into BS, pick up a bead and slide it to the bottom of the thread where it comes out of the DBH, needle over and then under the loop that led up to the group. Making sure that the working thread is lying under the needle; pull through to form a buttonhole stitch that lies horizontally below the group of two DBH stitches with the thread lying behind the bead. Miss 1 x BS]. Repeat [to] to end. Step down.
2. Working RL, 1 x DBH into each loop. Step down.
3. Repeat rows 1 and 2 until you have filled the entire shape.
4. To join it to the BS at the bottom come up from under the BS that forms the bottom edge, work the DBH stitch and go back into the fabric under the BS and thereafter, moving on to the next place you need to come up.
5. Referring to the instructions for working with twisted thread at the end of the embroidery stitches gallery, make a cord with a doubled over single strand of stranded cotton (see page 50).
6. Thread this cord onto a large chenille needle, come up from under the BS on one side of the rows that comprise single DBH stitches (row 2) and weave over and under the single DBH stitches worked in each and every row 2.

Dick wing-filler

PREPARATION
BS outline.

TOP ROW STITCH LENGTH:
To accommodate 2 x DBH.

1. Working LR, [1 x DBH into the 3rd BS, miss 2 BS]. Repeat [to] to end. Step down.
2. #working RL [4 x DBH into each large loop]. Repeat [to] to end. Step down.
3. Working LR, [miss large loop, 1 x DBH into each of the next 3 loops]. Repeat [to] to end. Step down.
4. Working RL, [miss large loop, 1 x DBH into each of the next 2 loops]. Repeat [to] to end. Step down.
5. Working LR, [miss large loop, 1 x DBH into the small loop]. Repeat [to] to end. Step down.
6. Working RL, 4 x DBH into each large loop. Step down.#

Keep working the rows from # to # until you have filled the required space. Following the instructions for the bottom row in the general tips, attach the detached buttonhole stitch at the bottom.

Referring to the project instructions to determine how many strands of thread you need to use and then to the instructions for working with twisted thread (see page 50), twist a length of cord. Thread the cord onto a 22 or 24 chenille needle and weave it over and under the single stitches in row 1 and thereafter in all the rows described as row 5 and shown in the diagram on the left.

I have suggested weaving with a chenille needle because you would need a large tapestry needle to accommodate the twisted thread and it really is so difficult to get a large tapestry needle through the fabric. So, use a chenille needle and be careful not to snag the existing needle lace as you weave each row.

Needle-weaving techniques

GENERAL INSTRUCTIONS

- All the weaving stitches in this gallery are variations of the same technique.
- **Always work in a hoop** to prevent puckering of the base fabric.
- Stitch the warp threads first.
- Referring to "warp" at the beginning of each stitch, determine the colour of the thread, whether there is more than one colour and, if so, how many warp stitches are to be worked in each of the colours.
- Once your warp stitches are in place, move on to "weft". Determine the colour or colours of thread that you will need to use and thread each colour separately on a tapestry needle.
- The pattern is formed in the weft stitches and it is in this part of the process that you will vary the basic pattern.
- Take note of the number of the row in each pattern repeat. These are the numbered rows and when you have worked all of them, return to the first row working as many pattern repeats as you need to fill the shape that you have.
- "O" means go over and "U" means go under one or more warp threads.
- If the beginning of the row has instructions in brackets, you only work these stitches at the beginning. When you reach the end of the instructions for that, return to and work from the instruction immediately after the closing bracket.
- Repeat the instructions until you reach the end of the row.
- Use a sharp embroidery needle to work the warp stitches and a blunt tapestry needle to weave the weft stitches.
- It is almost impossible to create a smooth edge to your weaving. Try to be as even and smooth as you can but be aware that you will need to either outline the area or cover the edge in some way. Crewel or needle-lace stitches, beads or beaded objects and tatting are suitable for this task.
- Once complete, woven areas are sufficiently stable to work simple embroidery over the top, e.g. fly stitch fronds can soften the shape.

The warp stitches

- Making sure that they start and end on the outline of the shape and using a sharp needle, these are long, straight stitches that go from the top edge of the shape to the bottom edge directly below, following the lines that demarcate the edge.
- The direction of the warp stitches will depend on what you want from the final weave. Usually, it is best to do the warp stitches over the shortest side of the shape but techniques that make a pattern, particularly a stripe, may need to be placed in a specific direction.
- Using the weaving techniques in this book to fill spaces in your embroidery will create an impression of fabric that has been appliquéd on the base fabric of your project. Do not be tempted to follow the shape that you wish to fill. It is important that these techniques are working vertically and horizontally at right angles to one another.
- Leave just a sliver of the base fabric showing through between the warp stitches. If you place them too close together, the final woven area will be too full and may bulge.
- Make sure that the warp stitches are taut.
- As a rule, it is usually easier to start in the centre of the shape, working to the left or right, then returning to the centre and working in the opposite direction. This tends to make it easier to keep the angle of the warp stitches vertical.

The weft stitches

- The weft stitches are worked with a tapestry needle, according to each individual pattern, at right angles to the weft stitches.
- It is the weft stitches that create the pattern in the weave.

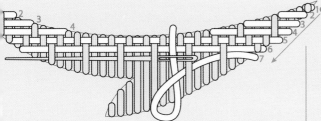

- Always start the weft stitches at the widest point of the shape. This could be at one end of the shape as depicted in the diagram above.

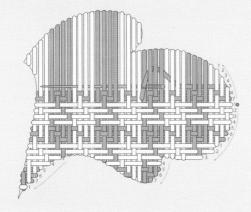

- Or, as is usually the case, it could be in the middle of the shape.
- When working from the middle of the shape, start on row 1 of the pattern (see Keeping the pattern intact on the right).
- Work as many pattern repeats as you need to until you reach the bottom of the shape. The pattern repeat in the diagram above is seven rows, so you are working from row 1 to row 7 each time.
- Return to the centre and work a reverse sequence of rows until you reach the top. This will mean that, in the diagram above, you will work from row 7 to row 1 each time.

Keeping the pattern intact

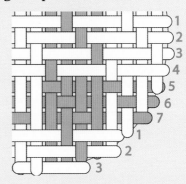

- Having started at the widest point of the shape, you will have to decrease as the shape changes. You will still, however, need to keep the pattern of the weaving intact and you do this by always counting from the first warp stitch, but only going over or under stitches as they become available. Using the above diagram as an example this should happen as follows:

Colour 2:

Row no.	Pattern	Count	Pick up from
Row 1	(O2, U1) O3, U1	-	Start of pattern
Row 2	(O1, U1) O3, U1	-	Start of pattern
Row 3	(U1) O3, U1	-	Start of pattern
Row 4	O3, U1	-	Start of pattern

Colour 1:

Row no.	Pattern	Count	Pick up from
Row 5	(U3) O1, U3	-	Start of pattern
Row 6	(U2) O1, U3	(U1)	(+U1) O1, U3
Row 7	(U1) O1, U3	(U1)	O1, U3

Colour 2:

Row no.	Pattern	Count	Pick up from
Row 1	(O2, U1) O3, U1	(O2, U1)	O3, U1
Row 2	(O1, U1) O3, U1	(O1, U1) O1	+O2, U1
Row 3	(U1) O3, U1	(U1) O3, U1	O3, U1

GENERAL TIPS – THE WEFT STITCHES

- Like the warp stitches, weft stitches should also be spaced about a thread's width apart.
- Weft stitches should be straight. If previous rows cause them to bow, your stitches are too close together.
- When working the first weft stitch, pull the thread straight before going into the fabric at the other end. This will determine where you need to go in on the other side.
- If you are right-handed, always work from right to left, going back to the right-hand side for the beginning of each row. It's impossible to work out where to start if you go backwards and forwards.
- If you're left-handed, work from left to right. It will not make any real difference to the pattern.
- This will mean that you will have long pieces of thread on the back of your work. So what.
- The tapestry needle works as the shuttle to guide the weft threads over and under the warp threads.
- Loom weavers use a tool called a 'beater'. It has teeth on the one side that are similar to a comb. This is used to push the weft thread up towards the previous weft thread at the end of each row. You will use your tapestry needle to do this.
- When working down, starting from the third row, as you go over and under the warp threads, push the needle up hard so that previous weft threads are pushed towards each other.
- When working in an upwards direction, as you go over and under the warp threads, push the needle down hard so that previous weft threads are pushed towards each other.
- The row that you are working on will always hang down a bit, but you should not be concerned as every row will eventually be pushed into place as you fill the space with weaving.
- If the row you are working on seems to not be fitting in as it should, it is usually because you have made a counting mistake in the previous row.

THE PATTERNS

Basic double-weaving

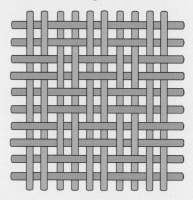

Warp: colour 1
Weft: colour 1 – or a different colour
(pattern repeat 4 rows)

1. O2, U2
2. O2, U2
3. U2, O2
4. U2, O2

Basic double-weaving – duck wing step 44

Warp: 2 x colour 1 #16 8327
2 x colour 2 #16 4000
2 x colour 3 #16 4379
2 x colour 2 #16 4000
2 x colour 1 #16 8327
2 x colour 4 #16 8083
2 x colour 1 #16 8327
2 x colour 2 #16 4000
2 x colour 1 #16 8327
2 x colour 3 #16 4379
2 x colour 1 #16 8327

2 x colour 2 #16 4000
2 x colour 1 #16 8327
2 x colour 4 #16 8083
Weft: 2 x colour 2 #16 4000
2 x colour 1 #16 8327

The bulk of the colour differentiation in the pattern occurs in the warp stitches as listed above with the pattern repeating after 14 pairs of stitches. The weft stitches are worked with only two colours as listed above.

Basic double-weaving – duck wing steps 67 and 71

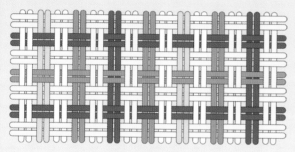

Warp: 2 x colour 1 #16 4000
2 x colour 2 #16 8083
2 x colour 3 #16 4000
2 x colour 2 #16 8327
2 x colour 1 #16 3000
2 x colour 4 #16 4379
2 x colour 1 #16 3000
2 x colour 2 #16 8327

Weft: 2 x colour 2 #16 4000
2 x colour 2 #16 8083
2 x colour 3 #16 4000
2 x colour 1 #16 8327

The bulk of the colour differentiation in the pattern occurs in the warp stitches as listed above with the pattern repeating after eight pairs of stitches. The weft stitches are worked with only three colours and the pattern repeating after four pairs of stitches, as listed above.

Basic single-weaving

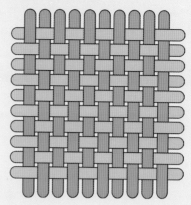

Warp: colour 1
Weft: colour 1 – or a different colour
(pattern repeat 2 rows)

1. O1, U1
2. U1, O1

Basic single-weaving – bird's leg variation

Warp: 1 x colour 2
4 x colour 1
Weft: colour 1

1. O1, U1
2. U1, O1

Checks and stripes no. 1

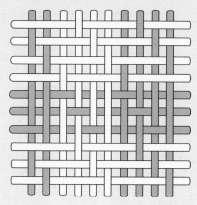

Warp: 4 x colour 1
4 x colour 2
Weft: 4 x colour 2
3 x colour 1 (pattern repeat 7 rows)

COLOUR 2
1. (O2, U1) O3, U1
2. (O1, U1) O3, U1
3. (U1) O3, U1
4. O3, U1

COLOUR 1
5. (U3) O1, U3
6. (U2) O1, U3
7. (U1) O1, U3

Checks and stripes no. 8

Warp: 4 x colour 1
4 x colour 2
Weft: 2 x colour 1
2 x colour 2 (pattern repeat 8 rows)

COLOUR 1
1. (U2) O2, U2
2. (U2) O2, U2
3. O2, U2
4. O2, U2

COLOUR 2
1. (U2) O2, U2
2. (U2) O2, U2
3. O2, U2
4. O2, U2

Checks and stripes no. 13

Warp: colour 1
Weft: colour 2
colour 3 (pattern repeat 4 rows

COLOUR 2
1. (U2) O2, U2
2. (U2) O2, U2

COLOUR 3
1. O2, U2
2. O2, U2

Checks and stripes no. 16

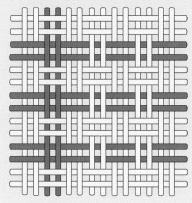

Warp: 10 x colour 1
        2 x colour 2
Weft: colour 1
        colour 2 (pattern repeat 4 rows)

COLOUR 1
1. U2 O2

COLOUR 2
1. O2, U2

Single weaving shading (see page 44)

Texture no. 2

Warp: colour 1
Weft: colour 2
      (pattern repeat 8 rows)

1. O1, U1
2. *(U1) O3, U1*

3. Repeat * to *
4. Repeat * to *
5. O1, U1
6. #(O2, U1) O3, U1#
7. Repeat # to #
8. Repeat # to #

Texture no. 2 – variation

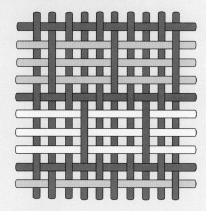

Warp: colour 1
Weft: colour 1
      colour 2
      colour 3 (pattern repeat 8 rows)

COLOUR 1
1. O1, U1

COLOUR 2
1. *(U1) O3, U1*
2. Repeat * to *
3. Repeat * to *

COLOUR 1
1. O1, U1

COLOUR 3
1. #(O2, U1) O3, U1#
2. Repeat # to #
3. Repeat # to #

Texture no. 3

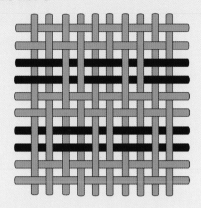

Warp: colour 1
Weft: colour 1
        colour 2 (pattern repeat 8 rows)

COLOUR 1
1. O1, U1
2. (U1) O1, U1

COLOUR 2
1. O2, U2
2. O2, U2

COLOUR 1
1. O1, U1
2. (U1) O1, U1

COLOUR 2
1. (U2) O2, U2
2. (U2) O2, U2

Texture no. 5 – 1

Warp: colour 1
Weft: colour 2 (pattern repeat 4 rows)

1. (O1, U2) O2, U2
2. (U2) O2, U2
3. (U1) O2, U2
4. O2, U2

Texture no. 5 – 2 (mirror image of 1)

Warp: colour 1
Weft: colour 2 (pattern repeat 4 rows)

1. (U1, O2) U2, O2
2. (U2) O2, U2
3. (O1) U2, O2
4. O2, U2

Texture no. 5 – variation

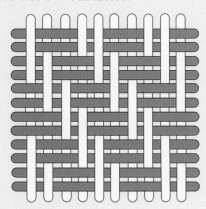

Warp: colour 1
Weft: colour 2(pattern repeat 8 rows)

1. (O1, U2) O2, U2
2. (O1, U2) O2, U2
3. (U2) O2, U2
4. (U2) O2, U2
5. (U1) O2, U2
6. (U1) O2, U2
7. O2, U2
8. O2, U2

Double-weaving twill with variation 1

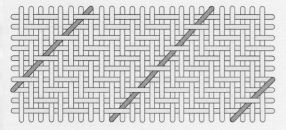

Based on texture no. 5 (see page 68), accentuate
some of the diagonal lines that form in the pattern
to emphasis the look of a feather. With a contrasting thread, come up at the edge adjacent to the
bottom of one set of diagonal pattern lines. Weave
over and under the horizontal weft stitches that
make up that diagonal pattern, to the top edge.
Missing two diagonal pattern lines, come up at the
top edge and weave downwards going over the
line where you went under before, and vice versa.

Double-weaving twill with variation 2

The diagram at the bottom of this page is a simplified version of how to do the double-woven twill in the pheasant's tail. It has been simplified in order to get sufficient detail into the space allowed but in such a way that you will understand the concept. Referring to the double-woven twill explained on page 69, and starting at the base of the tail feather:

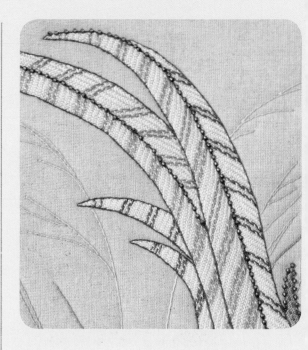

1. Weave a diagonal line through the weft stitches as indicated in the above illustration.

2. Weave a second diagonal line through the same diagonal line of weft stitches but where you went under with the first line, go over with this line, where you went over, go under.

3. Moving up the tail and working in through the very next diagonal line of weft stitches, repeat steps 1 and 2 creating a second double row of double weaving.

4. Moving up the tail, miss the next two sets of weft stitches and repeat. In some instances, you might miss two sets of weft stitches on the one side and three on the other. It is fine to do this. What is more important is that the stripes meet at the vein of the feather, in the middle, and that you are satisfied with the angle of those stripes. Use the colour image in the instructions for the project to guide you.

5. When you get towards the top of the tail feather and it starts to curve to the left, you will find that if you weave through only the weft stitches your stripe will be at the wrong angle. Referring to the two pairs of stripes on the right in the below diagram, weave over and under the weft stitches where possible.

Where this is not possible because of the angle you are aiming for, weave over and under the warp stitches.

It seems complicated but once you get started you will find that it isn't really. The important thing is the angle and, where you are working with two sides of the same feather, that those stripes should meet in the middle. Good luck!

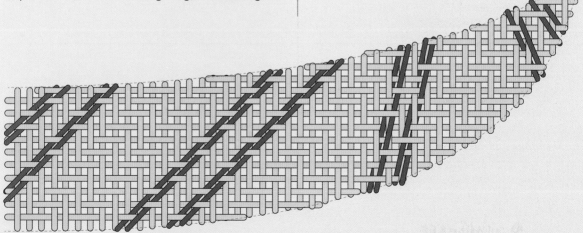

Weaving a twill feather

This is based on texture no. 5 (see page 68). To create a twill weave, you work the warp stitches in one colour as noted in the project instructions. Thereafter, using the colour noted in the project instructions, work rows of weft stitches. The sequence of each row is over two, under two, but as you do each row, the sequence starts either a warp stitch later or a warp stitch earlier, depending on which way you want to point the slant that forms in the weave. This is illustrated in the diagrams below, the lighter version being a mirror image of the first.

You will start on one side of the shape that needs to be filled, usually working from the base of the feather towards the tip and making sure that the diagonal slant that forms goes backwards, towards the vein. When you reach approximately the centre of the shape, what you consider to be where the vein of the feather would be, change the direction of the diagonal slant to go forwards towards the tip.

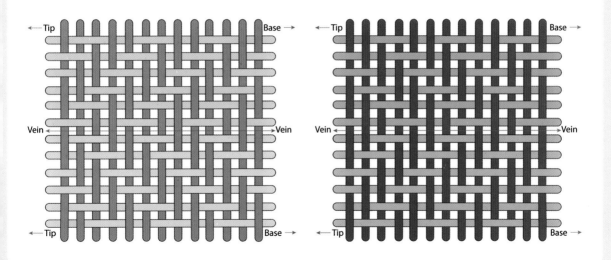

Texture no. 9

Warp: colour 1

Weft: colour 1 or 2 (pattern repeat 6 rows)

1. (U3) O1, U3
2. (U3) O1, U3
3. (U3) O1, U3
4. O3, U1
5. O3, U1
6. O3, U1

Claude

A fanciful take on the mythological phoenix or firebird, the design measures 260 x 320 mm (10¼ x 12½") and includes the use of a wide range of interesting techniques and stitches

Materials

Fabric

450 x 450 mm (18 x 18") medium-weight cotton-twill base fabric, colour Ecru

450 x 450 mm (18 x 18") off-white cotton-voile backing fabric x 2

450 x 450 mm (18 x 18") 100 gsm polyester or cotton batting

Embroidery Frame

2 pairs 17" Edmunds stretcher bars

Needles

Size 7 Embroidery needles
Size 10 Embroidery needles
Size 11 Bead-embroidery needles
Size 24 Tapestry needles
Size 26 Tapestry needles

Threads and Beads

DMC STRANDED COTTON

1420	Hazelnut Brown
422	Light Hazelnut Brown
561	Very Dark Celadon Green
564	Very Light Jade
597	Turquoise
598	Light Turquoise
869	Very Dark Hazelnut Brown
912	Light Emerald Green
917	Medium Plum
3607	Light Plum
3608	Very Light Plum
3609	Ultra Light Plum
3808	Ultra Very Dark Turquoise x 2
3810	Dark Turquoise
3828	Golden Brown
3855	Light Autumn Gold
3865	Winter White
3866	Ultra Very Light Mocha Brown x 2
4030	Monet's Garden x 2

DMC DENTELLES #80

3688	Medium Mauve
954	Nile Green

PRECENSIA FINCA PERLE #12

3664	Dark Turquoise
3000	Ecru
2240	Mauve

DI VAN NIEKERK HAND-PAINTED SILK RIBBON

2mm 77 Off-white

MADEIRA GLAMOUR #12 METALLIC THREAD

3037 Jade Green

MIYUKI SIZE 15° BEADS

2425 Silver Lined Teal (4 g)

PRECIOSA VIVA 12 FLAT-BACK CRYSTALS

2 pieces 20ss Smoke Topaz AB

General instructions

- Refer to the general project instructions on page 19.

Stitching instructions

*Throughout this design you will be instructed to finish off sections with outlines. This will be done with stitches as described in each section, but you should not work these outlines until all surrounding embroidery has been done.

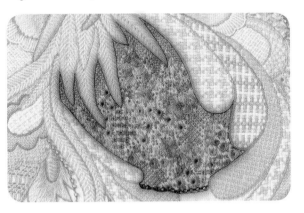

1. Using a single strand of 4030, fill Claude's belly with freestyle stitching (see page 38) and working the following stitches: Ox-head stitch; buttonhole circles; buttonhole flowers; single-weaving shading; trellis couching – basic diagonal; trellis couching with cross stitch filling; sheaf stitch; eye-stitch variation; three-petal lazy daisy bud; nine-petal lazy daisy flower; buttonhole foxglove stem; French knot.

2. *Outline the bottom edge of the freestyle-stitched belly with beaded backstitch using two strands of 3808 and beads 15° 2425.

3. Moving to the top right area of the belly, fill the first shape with needle-weaving checks and stripes no. 8. Use perle #12 threads, 2240 for colour 1 and 3000 for colour 2. *Outline with whipped back-stitch using two strands of 917.

4. Fill the next shape with needle-weaving checks and stripes no. 16. Use perle #12 threads, 3000 for colour 1 and 3664 for colour 2. *Outline with whipped backstitch using two strands of 3808.

5. Fill the next shape with satin stitch that runs from left to right over the shortest side using two strands of 422. Using a single strand of 3828, work vertical and horizontal trellis couching over the satin stitch. Work the long straight stitches that go horizontal to the satin stitch first. *Outline with whipped backstitch using two strands of 420.

6. Fill the next shape with pink checks as instructed in step 3 above.

7. Fill the shape that hides behind the others with single-weaving shading using a single strand of 4030. *Outline the top edge with whipped back-stitch using two strands of 3808.

8. Fill the next shape with satin stitch and trellis couching as instructed in step 5 above.

9. Fill the next shape with pink checks as instructed in step 3 above.

10. Fill the next shape with teal stripes as instructed in step 4 above.

11. Moving to the left side of the belly, work those crescent shapes as follows, from the top:
- as instructed in step 3;
- as instructed in step 5;
- as instructed in step 3;
- as instructed in step 4.

12. Moving to the lower neck-feathers, these are all worked with fly stitch variation as detailed below. *Outline each one with outline stitch.

	Fly stitch two strands	Straight stitch two strands	Outline single strand
Bottom left	3855	3828	420
Bottom right	564	912	561
Top far left	3855	3828	420
Top 2 small pink	3609	3607	917
Top 3 large pink	3609	3607	917
Top 4 green	564	912	561
Top 5 pink	3609	3607	917
Top 6 green	564	912	561
Top 7 yellow	3828	3855	420

13. Moving to the upper neck-feathers and starting from the far left, work satin stitch over the shortest side of this feather using two strands of 564. With a single strand of 912, work fine backstitch adjacent to the satin stitch on both sides of the feather down to the tip. Using a single strand of the same thread, work interlaced herringbone stitch through the backstitch on either side. *Outline with outline stitch using a single strand of 561.

14. Work the next feather to the right with fly stitch variation as in step 12, using the 3855, 3828 and 420 thread combination.

15. Work the next feather to the right, at the bottom, with fly stitch variation as in step 12, using the 564, 912 and 561 thread combination.

16. The one above that is worked with satin stitch and interlaced herringbone as described in step 13 above. Use 598 for the satin stitch, 597 for the backstitch and herringbone and 3808 for the outline.

17. The next three feathers to the right, which abut the head, are worked with satin stitch and interlaced herringbone. The first one uses the green combination as in step 13 above, the next one uses the teal colour combination described in step 16 above, and the far-right feather repeats the green combination as in step 13 above.

18. The remaining upper-neck feathers which peep out from under the ones just described are filled with two-strand satin stitch worked over the shortest side. Thereafter, work single-strand fly stitch from tip to base over the satin stitch.

*Outline with single strand outline stitch. Use the threads listed in the table below:

	Satin stitch	Fly stitch	Outline stitch
Left pink	3609	3607	917
Middle yellow	3855	422	420
Right pink	3608	3607	917

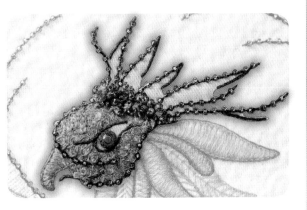

19. Following the guidelines for two-tone vermicelli couching (see page 49), leaving the eye clear, fill the bird's face using two strands of 4030 couched down with a single strand. Do the second stage with a single strand couched down with a single strand. Let the shading happen naturally.

20. Pad the beak with stem stitch running along the length of the shape, using two strands of 3855. Thereafter working in the opposite direction, do satin stitch over the padding using a single strand of the same thread. Outline the beak with backstitch using a single strand of 3828. Using a single strand of the same thread, work interlaced herringbone stitch through the backstitch on either side. *Outline with outline stitch using a single strand of 420.

21. Following the guidelines for the caged flatback crystal (see page 53), attach the 20ss smoked topaz AB flat-back crystal to the centre of the eye using a single strand of 869. Work the lines of the eye with whipped backstitch using two strands of 3808, taking the needle through the two-tone vermicelli stitch where the lines go into the face.

22. Work the short line below the beak in the same way. With a single strand of 4030, work loose-wrap French knots to soften the edge of the face below the beak.

23. *Outline the lower and upper edges of the face with beaded backstitch using a doubled-over strand of 3808 and bead 15° 2425.

24. Moving to the crest plumage and using the colour image as your guide, work most of the lines with beaded backstitch using a doubled-over strand of 3808 and bead 15° 2425. The plain lines are worked with whipped backstitch using two strands of 3808.

25. Between the base of the crest plumage and the top of the head, work a mass of beaded drizzle stitches following the guidelines in the bead embroidery gallery (see page 52). Vary the number of cast-on stitches between five and ten, using two strands of 4030 and bead 15° 2425.

Moving to the right-hand side wing, these instructions also apply to the upper two thirds of the left-hand side wing, which is a mirror image of the wing described. The lower one third of the left-hand side wing will be described in due course.

26. Starting on the left, in the corner, fill the yellow area with long and short stitch. Start at the base with 3828 shading through 422 to 3855 at the top.

27. Using two strands of 3865, pad the scalloped shape adjacent to the yellow area with stem stitch.

Work striped blanket stitch over the padding using perle #12 3000 for the blanket stitch and 2240 for the straight stitches in between.

28. Using two strands of 420, work a line of the backstitch/French knot combination (see page 27) in the ditch between the long and short stitch and the striped blanket stitch. *Outline the outer edge of the blanket stitch with single strand outline stitch using 917.

29. Moving to the shapes outside of the striped blanket stitch, fill the middle one with battlement couching. Working with two strands throughout, do the first layer with 3810, follow with 597 and 598 and work the couching stitch with 3809. *Outline the outer edge with beaded backstitch using two strands of 3808 and bead 15° 2425.

30. Fill the middle of the shapes on either side of the battlement-couched area with woven trellis-couching using perle #12 3000 for shade 1, the trellis. Use two strands of 564 for shade 2, the couching stitches, and perle #12 3000 for shades 3 and 4, the weaving.

31. Pad the outside area of each of these shapes with stem stitch lines running the length of the area using two strands of 3866. With a single strand of the same threadwork satin stitch over and in the opposite direction to the padding. Outline the top and bottom edges of the satin stitch with fine backstitch using Dentelles #80 3688. Working from the outside edge into the middle, do needle-lace stitch no. 2 over the padding anchoring the stitches to the backstitch at top and bottom. When the needle lace is complete, whip the anchoring backstitches at top and bottom and finally, *outline the outer edge with outline stitch using a single strand of 917. Using the same thread, work a line of outline stitch in the ditch between the needle-lace edge and the woven trellis middle of the motif.

32. Pad the yellow feather at the top with lines of stem stitch that run the length of the shape using two strands of 3855. With a single strand of the same thread, work satin stitch over the padding. This should run in the opposite direction to the padding. With a single strand of 422, work fly stitch over the satin stitch from tip to base. *Outline the bottom edge with outline stitch using a single strand of 420.

33. The inner edge of the wing is outlined with beaded backstitch using a doubled-over strand of 3808 and bead 15° 2425. Don't do this yet, rather leaving it until you have completed the entire wing and do it as a continuous line with the rest of the beaded backstitch on the inner edge of the wing.

34. Moving out to the edge of the wing and referring to the image above, fill the bottom motif with eye-stitch variation using a single strand of 4030. *Outline the visible edges with whipped backstitch using two strands of 3808. Stitch single beads 15° 2425 on the outside edge of the bottom line, curving around to the tip. Use a doubled-over single strand of 3866.

35. Moving up to the next motif, fill the middle area with needle-lace Claude filler no. 1 (see page 59). Start at the tip, doing the first detached buttonhole stitch of the group of two stitches into the backstitch on the one side, and the second in the backstitch on the other side of the point. Use Dentelles #80 954 for the needle-lace stitches and Madeira #12 3037 to weave. When you have completed the needle-laced centre, whip the backstitch around the edges with the Dentelles thread. *Outline the visible edges with outline stitch using a single strand of 561.

36. Fill the outer part of this motif with shaded long and short stitch facing into the middle. Using single strands, start towards the tip with the inside shade 597 shading through 598 to 564 on the outside. Work a line of beaded backstitch up the centre line that forms the vein, using a doubled-over strand of 3808 and bead 15° 2425. *Outline the visible edges with outline stitch using a single strand of 561.

37. The two yellow feathers are filled with fly-stitch variation using two strands of cotton. For the bottom shape use 420 for the fly stitch and 3828 for the straight stitches. The top shape uses 3855 for the fly stitch and 420 for the straight stitches. *Outline the visible edges of both shapes with outline stitch using a single strand of 420.

38. The shape to the left of the yellow feathers is filled with Claude needle-lace filler no. 2 (see page 59). Use Dentelles 954 for the backstitch and the needle-lace stitches, Madeira 3037 for the single-strand weaving and Di van Niekerk 2 mm silk ribbon 77 for the insertion row. When you have completed the needle-laced centre, whip the backstitch around the edges with the Dentelles thread. *Outline the visible edges with outline stitch using a single strand of 561.

39. The bottom of the next motif is filled with fly-stitch variation using 3608 for the fly stitch and 3607 for the straight stitch. Outline the visible edge with outline stitch using a single strand of 917.

40. The top of the motif is filled with basic double-weaving (see page 64) using perle #12 3664 for the warp stitch and 3000 for the weft stitches. Outline the outside edge with whipped backstitch using two strands of 3808. Work a line of beaded backstitch up the vein between the two sides of the motif using a doubled-over strand of 3808 and bead 15° 2425.

41. Starting on the inside section depicted in the image above, fill the far-left area with needle-weaving checks and stripes no. 16 (see page 67). Use perle #12 threads, 3000 for colour 1 and 3664 for colour 2. *With reference to the image above, outline the visible lines with whipped backstitch using two strands of 3808.

42. The inner edge of the wing is outlined with beaded backstitch using a doubled-over strand of 3808 and bead 15° 2425. Don't do this yet, rather leaving it until you have completed the entire wing and do it as a continuous line with the rest of the beaded backstitch on the inner edge of the wing.

43. Moving to the areas at the bottom, fill the semi-circular areas, continuing to the pointed tip with freestyle stitching as described in step 1 (see page 75) for the belly of the bird. *Outline the visible lines with whipped backstitch using two strands of 3808.

44. Fill the small yellow feather with fly stitch variation using two strands each of 3855 for the fly stitch and 422 for the straight stitch. *Outline the visible lines with outline stitch using a single strand of 420.

45. The middle of the remaining area is filled with single weaving shading using a single strand of 4030.

46. Referring to the table on page 80 for thread numbers, fill the ovate shapes with vertical satin stitch padding done with two strands and overlaid with horizontal satin stitch worked with a single strand. Using a single strand, surround the satin stitch with backstitch through which you should work interlaced herringbone stitch. To complete each ovate shape, whip the backstitch with one strand of the thread noted in the table.

Starting from the tip and working downwards:

	Satin stitch	Backstitch and interlaced herringbone stitch	Whipping
Top yellow	3855	422	420
Top pink	3609	3607	917
Green	564	912	561
Bottom yellow	3855	422	420
Bottom pink	3609	3607	917

47. Using two strands of 3865, pad the pink scalloped shapes on either side of the weaving with stem stitch. Work striped blanket stitch over the padding using perle #12 3000 for the blanket stitch and 2240 for the straight stitches in between. *Outline the outer edge, outside the blanket stitch, with outline stitch using a single strand of 917. Using the same thread, work outline stitch in the ditch at the base of the striped blanket stitch.

48. The remaining edge outside the single-weave inside, that goes to the tip, is filled with double blanket stitch. Start at the tip with the first layer using two strands of 564, forming the ridge or purl on the upper side. When you reach the point where the edge splits, continue working the upper side. Return to the point where the split occurred and work the lower side with the ridge or purl edge on the upper side, facing into the middle against the single weaving. Using two strands of 3808, work the next layer from the tip with the ridge or purl edge facing downwards. When you reach the split, continue with the lower section and return to the split to work the upper section, with the purl edge facing down into the middle against the single weaving.

49. *Outline the outer edge, outside the blanket stitch, with outline stitch using a single strand of 3808. Stitch single beads 15° 2425 on the outside edge of the bottom line, curving around to the tip. Use a doubled-over single strand of 3866.

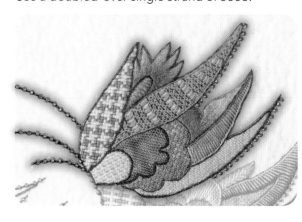

50. Moving to the top section of the wing, starting with the bottom, inner motif fill the bottom, middle area with basic double-weaving using perle #12 3000. To add the green colour, weave a single strand of Dentelles #80 954 just below the first warp and the first weft stitch of each pair of stitches, following the same weaving sequence. *Outline the outer edge with whipped backstitch using two strands of 3808.

51. Fill the area above that with single weaving shading using a single strand of 4030. *Outline the visible outer edge with whipped backstitch using two strands of 3808.

52. Fill the area above and around that with stem stitch padding running the length of the area and using two strands of 3866. With a single strand of the same thread, work satin stitch over and in the opposite direction to the padding, fanning slightly as you go around the shape. Outline the top and bottom edges of the satin stitch with fine backstitch, using Dentelles #80 3688. Working from the outside edge into the middle, do needlelace stitch no. 2 over the padding, anchoring the stitches to the backstitch at top and bottom. When the needle lace is complete, whip the anchoring backstitches at top and bottom and finally, *outline the outer edge with outline stitch using a single strand of 917.

53. Moving outwards and starting with the lowest feather shape, fill the area with woven trellis couching using perle #12 3000 for shade 1, the trellis. Use two strands of 564 for shade 2, the couching stitches and perle #12 3000 for shades 3 and 4, the weaving. *Outline the visible edge with whipped backstitch using two strands of 561. Stitch single beads 15° 2425 on the outside edge of the bottom line, curving around to the tip. Use a doubled-over single strand of 3866.

54. Moving up, fill the feather shape above that with double blanket stitch. Start from the tip with the purl edge facing to the top using two strands of 3810. Work the second layer with the purl edge facing down using two strands of 564. *Outline the entire outer edge with outline stitch using a single strand of 3808.

55. Moving up, fill the next shape with long and short stitch shading starting at the base with a single strand of 3828 shading through 422 to 3855 at the tip. *Outline the upper edge with outline stitch using a single strand of 420.

56. Moving up to the next shape, fill this with Claude needle-lace filler no. 2 (see step 38, page 79). Finally, stitch single beads 15° 2425 on the outside edge of the bottom line, curving around to the tip. Use a doubled-over single strand of 3866.

57. Moving to the shape above and slightly to the left of the needle-laced area, pad the ovate shape at bottom centre with vertical satin stitch using two strands of 598. With a single strand of the same thread, work horizontal satin stitch over the padding. Using a single strand of 597, surround the satin stitch with backstitch through which you should work interlaced herringbone stitch. To complete each ovate shape, whip the backstitch with one strand of the same thread and finally, *outline the shape adjacent to the whipped backstitch with a single strand of 3808.

58. Before you do that outline, fill the remainder of this motif with long and short stitch shading starting at the base with a single strand of 3810 shading through 597 to 564 at the tips. *Outline the visible edges with outline stitch using a single strand of 561.

59. Moving to the final motif at the top of the wing, fill the area with pink checks as instructed in step 3 (see page 75).

60. Work beaded backstitch on the remaining fine lines, continuing as mentioned previously, down the line that forms the edge of the inner wing until you reach the pink checked area of the outer belly on the right-hand wing and the neck feathers on the left-hand wing.

Save for the bottom area of the left-hand wing, instructions for which are below, repeat steps 26 to 60 to complete the left wing. You will be working a mirror image of what you have already done.

61. Starting with the inside motif at the top, fill the middle area with basic double-weaving using perle #12 3000. To add the green colour, weave a single strand of Dentelles #80 954 just below the first warp and the first weft stitch of each pair of stitches, following the same weaving sequence. *Outline the outer edge with whipped backstitch using two strands of 3808.

62. Fill the area outside that with single weaving shading using a single strand of 4030. *Outline the visible outer edge with whipped backstitch using two strands of 3808.

63. Fill the area around that with stem stitch padding running the length of the area and using two strands of 3866. With a single strand of the same thread, work satin stitch over and in the opposite direction to the padding, fanning slightly as you go around the shape. Outline the top and bottom edges of the satin stitch with fine backstitch using Dentelles #80 3688. Working from the outside edge into the middle, do needle-lace stitch no. 2 over the padding anchoring the stitches to the backstitch at top and bottom. When the needle lace is complete, whip the anchoring backstitches at top and bottom and finally, *outline the outer edge with outline stitch using a single strand of 917.

64. Moving towards the bottom of the wing and starting on the left, fill the left side of the first motif with double blanket stitch. Start from the tip with the purl edge facing to the right using two strands of 3810. Work the second layer with the purl edge facing to the right using two strands of 564. *Outline the entire outer edge with outline stitch using a single strand of 3808.

65. Moving to the right, fill the remainder of the motif with long and short stitch shading starting at the base with a single strand of 3828 shading through 422 to 3855 at the tip. *Outline the outer edge with outline stitch using a single strand of 420.

66. Moving up to the next shape, fill this with Claude needle-lace filler no. 2 as instructed in step 38 (see page 79).

67. Moving to the remaining motif on the right, pad the ovate shape in the centre with vertical satin stitch using two strands of 598. With a single strand of the same thread, work horizontal satin stitch over the padding. Using a single strand of 597, surround the satin stitch with backstitch through which you should work interlaced herringbone stitch. To complete each ovate shape, whip the backstitch with one strand of the same thread and finally, *outline the shape adjacent to the whipped backstitch with a single strand of 3808.

68. Work the line that starts on the right edge of

the pink needle lace and continues down to the outside of the wing adjacent to the yellow fly-stitched feather with beaded backstitch, using a doubled-over stand of 3808 and bead 15° 2425.

69. Fill the left side of each tail feather, along with the bottom side after the curve, with needle-weaving texture no. 5 variation (see page 69). Use Perle #12 3000 for colour 1, the warp stitch and Perle #12 3664 for colour 2, the weft stitches.

70. Fill the right side of each tail feather, along with the top side after the curve, with eye-stitch variation using a single strand of 4030.

71. Outline the outer edges on both sides of each feather with whipped backstitch using two strands of 3808. *Work a line of beaded backstitch up the middle line or vein of each feather using a doubled-over strand of 3803 and beads 15° 2425.

72. Moving to the eyespot of each feather, fill the centre with Claude needle-lace filler no. 2 as instructed in step 38 (see page 79).

73. Fill the outer edge of the eyespot by working fly-stitch variation on each of the lines depicted. Start at the tip using two strands of 3855 for the fly stitch and two strands of 3828 for the straight stitches that lie in between. Thereafter, work a pair

– one on either side of the line at the top – using two strands of 420 for the fly stitch and two strands of 3828 for the straight stitches. Continue down each side alternating the 3855/2828 and 422/3828 combinations. Using a single strand of 420, work a line of outline stitch between each pair of fly stitch lines, where they meet.

If you are intending to turn this project into the page of a book as I have done, and you did not add the batting and additional voile backing from the beginning, you should now remove the project from the frame.

Place a layer of voile, then a layer of batting, then the project so far back over the frame and secure it all together, making sure that you stretch all of the layers as you go. There should be no folds visible on the back of the work. Everything should be smooth and well secured.

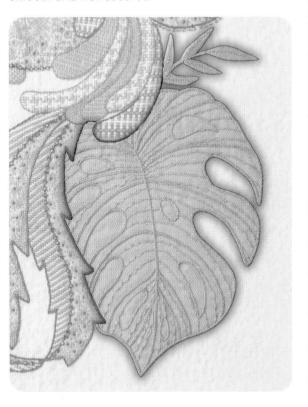

74. Starting with the main, delicious monster, leaf and using two strands of 3866 throughout, work:
• reverse chain stitch on all the solid lines;
• running stitch on all the dotted lines;
• whipped chain stitch on the circular shapes that depict the holes normally found in such a leaf.

75. Still using two strands of 3866, work the leaves on the fronds radiating from the large leaf with fly stitch. Using the same thread, work the main stems and any smaller stems that go into the main stem with whipped backstitch.

76. If you are quilting this project to make up the page of a book – or if you want to make the background more interesting - work meandering running stitch over the entire background using a single strand of 3866. Make sure that you take it into all the little nooks and crannies between the feathers and the leaves of the delicious monster.

Colin

Called everything from chicks to chooks, fowls to inkukhu, the chicken is the most widespread of the domesticated animals. Mostly kept as a source of food, there are many varieties of chicken and this rooster is a fanciful combination of those varieties. The project measures 310 x 280 mm (12¼ x 11").

Materials

Fabric

450 x 450 mm (18 x 18") cotton-linen blend base
    fabric in a natural colour
450 x 450 mm (18 x 18") off-white cotton-voile
    backing fabric x 2
450 x 450 mm (18 x 18") 100 gsm polyester or
    cotton batting

Embroidery frame

2 pairs 17" Edmunds stretcher bars

Needles

Size 7 Embroidery needles
Size 10 Embroidery needles
Size 11 Sharps quilting needles
Size 24 Tapestry needles
Size 26 Tapestry needles

Threads and beads

DMC STRANDED COTTON

Ecru	Ecru
311	Medium Navy Blue
407	Dark Desert Sand
433	Medium Brown
434	Light Brown
435	Very Light Brown
436	Tan
437	Light Tan
498	Dark Red
517	Dark Wedgewood
543	Ultra Very Light Beige Brown
632	Ultra Very Dark Desert Sand
646	Dark Beaver Grey
648	Light Beaver Grey
738	Very Light Tan
739	Ultra Very Light Tan
754	Light Peach
758	Very Light Terracotta
760	Salmon
761	Light Salmon
839	Dark Beige Brown
842	Very Light Beige Brown
3328	Dark Salmon
3712	Medium Salmon
3760	Medium Wedgewood
3765	Very Dark Peacock Blue
3772	Very Dark Desert Sand
3778	Light Terracotta
3830	Terracotta
3831	Dark Raspberry
3832	Medium Raspberry
3834	Dark Grape
3835	Medium Grape
3836	Light Grape
3842	Dark Wedgwood
3847	Dark Teal Green
3848	Medium Teal Green
3849	Light Teal Green
3851	Light Bright Green
45136	Black Forest

DMC SATIN THREAD

943   Medium Aquamarine

DMC PERLE #12

Ecru   Ecru
437   Light Tan
842   Very Light Beige Brown

FINCA PERLE #12

8026   Light Cocoa
8080   Very Dark Coffee Brown

DMC DENTELLES #80

ECRU   Ecru
437   Light Tan

MADEIRA GLAMOUR #12 METALLIC THREAD

3037   Jade Green
3229   Bronze

MIYUKI BEADS

2g   11° 579   Smoky Light Rose SL Alabaster
2g   15° 4249   SL Rose Bronze
2g   15° 2422F   Matte SL Topaz
2g   15° 641   Rose Bronze SL Alabaster
2g   15° 2425   Silver Lined Teal

PRECIOSA VIVA 12 FLAT-BACK CRYSTALS

1 piece 20ss Smoke Topaz AB

General instructions

- Refer to the general project instructions on page 19.

Stitching instrucxtions

*Throughout this design you will be instructed to finish off sections with outlines. This is done with stitches as described in each section only once all the surrounding embroidery has been completed.

1. Using a single strand of 4516, fill the lower part of Colin's belly with freestyle stitching (see page 38) and working the following stitches: buttonhole circles; buttonhole flowers; single weaving shading; diagonal trellis couching; trellis couching with cross-stitch filling; sheaf stitch; eye-stitch variation; three-petal lazy daisy bud; French knot. *Outline the bottom edge of the belly with whipped backstitch, using two strands of 839.

2. Fill the feather below the belly and on the left with long and short stitch shading. Using a single strand, start at the base of the feather with 3772 shading through 407 to 543 at the tip. With a single strand of 632, work fly stitch over the shading, starting at the tip and working down to the base. *Outline the feather with outline stitch using a single strand of the same thread.

3. The feather to the right is filled with beaded wheatear-stitch variation (see page 53) using a doubled-over strand of 3760 and bead 15° 2425. Use a single strand of Madeira 3037 to work the straight stitches on the side. *Outline the visible edges of the feather with outline stitch using a single strand of 3760.

4. Moving to the feathers on the top right side of the belly, work each one with long and short stitch shading. Using a single strand, start at the base of the feather with 3772 shading through 407 to 543 at the tip. *Outline the feather with outline stitch using a single strand of 632.

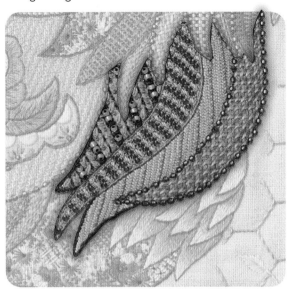

5. Moving to the area above and to the right, as highlighted in the image above, start on the left. Work a line of knotted cable-chain stitch on each of the dotted lines. Use two strands of 632 and bead 11° 579. Using a single strand of satin 943, work a line of backstitch down the middle of the space between the cable-chain lines. Using the colour image as your guide and with two strands of 738, work diagonal detached chain-stitch petals that seem to come out of the green stem in the centre. With two strands of 407, work a single French knot in the spaces between the petals. Couch a line of Madeira 3229 between the knotted cable-chain stitches and the detached chain petals. *Outline the visible edges of this feather with whipped backstitch using two strands of 632.

6. Outline the feather to the right of the one you have just worked with backstitch in Dentelles #80 437. Include the lines that go up into the point at the top. Following to the instructions for Colin Filler no. 1 (see page 60) and working from the base of the feather (where it comes out of those

above it) to the tip, use Dentelles #80 for the needle lace, bead 15° 2422F and DMC perle #12 Ecru for the twisted cord. When you have completed the inside, needle-laced area, whip the backstitches around the feather. *Outline the visible edges of this feather with outline stitch using a single strand of 434.

7. Fill the feather to the right of the one you have just done with needle-weaving texture no. 5 – 2 (see page 68). Use DMC perle #12 Ecru for the warp stitches which should be done over the short side and DMC perle #12 437 for the weft stitches which run the length of the feather. When you have filled the feather and following the directions for double-weaving twill with variation 1 (see page 69), accentuate the diagonal pattern using Finca perle #12 8026. *Outline the visible edges of this feather with whipped backstitch using two strands of 632.

8. Fill the feather to the right and on the outside of Colin's chest with trellis couching – woven (see page 47). Use two strands throughout, 437 for shade 1 and 738 for shade 2. Use 407 for shade 3 and 3772 for shade 4. *Outline the visible edges of this feather with beaded backstitch using a doubled-over strand of 434 and bead 15° 2422F.

9. Starting with the shape on the left in the image at the bottom of page 88, using two strands of 407, work trellis couching over the background area. Work beaded backstitch on the small curved 'tendril' that comes out of the left side, using a doubled-over strand of 839 and bead 15° 4249. *Outline the visible edges of the shape with whipped backstitch using two strands of 632.

10. Both of the purple check flowers are worked in the same way. Do horizontal satin stitch padding in the centre of the flower using two strands of DMC stranded cotton Ecru. With a single strand of the same thread do vertical satin stitch over the padding. Fill the petal area of both flowers with needle-weaving checks and stripes no. 13 (see page 66) using two strands of 3836 for colour 1, the warp stitches. Use two strands each of 3835 for colour 2 and stranded cotton Ecru for colour 3 when working the weft stitches. *Outline the visible edges of the petals and the outer edge of the flower centre with whipped backstitch using two strands of 3834. Whilst I would usually choose a perle thread to work needle weaving, sometimes the colour you want is not available in the perle ranges. I will then use stranded cotton and restrict the pattern I use to one that is simple.

11. Fill the ovate leaves within this shape with long and short stitch shading using a single strand of thread. Start at the base with 3847 shading through 3848 and 3849, then back through 3848 to 3847. With a single strand of 3847, work fly stitch over the shading, starting at the tip and working down to the base. *Outline each leaf with outline stitch using a single strand of 3847.

12. Moving to the right, fill the next shape with long lines of layered buttonhole stitch. Start with a short row in the left corner adjacent to the previous shape using two strands of 632. With the same thread, work the second row along the full length of the shape. Thereafter work two rows each along the full length of the shape using 3772, 407 and 543. Work the last row as an outline row as described in the embroidery stitch gallery) see page 31) using two strands of 632. *Outline the

remaining visible edge on the left with whipped backstitch using two strands of 632.

13. Moving to the right, fill the feather that peeps out from underneath with freestyle embroidery as described in step 1 (see page 87) using a single strand of 4516. *Outline the visible bottom edges with whipped backstitch using two strands of 839.

14. Moving right, fill the next feather with raised chain-stitch – woven (see page 43). Use two strands of 3772 for the raised chain-stitches and 407 to do the weaving. *Outline the visible edges with whipped backstitch using two strands of 632.

15. Moving to the lower feather that peeps out at the bottom and referring to chain stitch – interlaced variation 1 (see page 34), use two strands of 3760 for the chain and side straight-stitches and two strands of 3851 for the interlacing. *Outline the visible edges with whipped backstitch using two strands of 517.

16. Fill the feather to the right of the one you have just completed with trellis couching – woven (see page 47). Use two strands throughout, 407 for shade 1 and 3772 for shade 2. Use 543 for shades 3 and 4. *Outline the visible edges of this feather with beaded backstitch using a doubled-over strand of 632 and bead 15° 4249.

17. The next little feather is filled with needle-weaving checks and stripes no. 13 (see page 66). Using DMC perle #12 842 for colour 1, work the warp stitches horizontally over the shortest side, with the weft stitches worked along the length of the feather using Finca perle #12 8080 for colour 2 and Finca perle #12 8026 for colour 3. *Outline the visible bottom edges with whipped backstitch using two strands of 839.

18. Moving to the right, the next feather is filled with chain stitch – interlaced variation 1. Using two strands, the chain stitch and side straight stitches are done with 407 and the interlacing is worked with 632. *Outline both sides of the feather with beaded backstitch using a doubled-over single strand of 632 and bead 15° 641.

19. Moving to the right, the last feather highlighted in the image above is filled with layered buttonhole. Working with two strands and starting adjacent to the feather on the left, do two rows each with 632, 3772 and 407. The final row that forms the outline is worked with 632. *Outline the remaining visible edges with whipped backstitch using two strands of 632.

20. Starting below and to the left of the eye, fill the two scallop-shaped sections at the bottom with long and short stitch shading using a single strand of thread. Starting from the base and working to the tip of each section, the upper shape, closer to the eye starts with 3831 shading through 3832

and 437 to 738 at the tip. The lower shape uses 498 shading through 437 to 738. With a single strand of 738, work continuous trellis couching with cross-stitch filling over both shaded scallop shapes. *Outline the outside edge of each scallop with whipped backstitch using two strands of 839, stitching over the trellis that lies in the ditch between the two shapes.

21. Fill the red section above the scallops with trellis with cross-stitch couching variation 1 (see page 46), using a single strand of 498. Work it closely to create a solid-looking fill. *Outline the bottom edge with whipped backstitch using two strands of the same thread.

22. Use a single strand of DMC stranded cotton Ecru and fill both top and bottom of the irregular shape around the eye with single-weaving shading (see page 44). *Outline the outside edges with small reverse chain-stitch using a single strand of 739 and work outline stitch on the outside and adjacent to the chain with a single strand of 433.

23. To form the eye, follow the instructions for caging a 20ss flat-back crystal (see page 53) and attach a 20ss Smoke Topaz AB crystal on the larger circle in the centre of the eye using a single strand of 433. Fill the remainder of the semi-circle with a line or two of split backstitch using two strands of 434. *Outline the bottom of the semi-circle with outline stitch using a single strand of 433. Now pad what I am loosely going to call the eyebrow that runs over and beyond the eye with stem stitch using two strands of 437. Leaving enough space for two straight stitches in between, work short, vertical bullion knots over the padding using a single strand of 434. With two strands of 437, work two vertical straight stitches between each pair of bullion knots. *Outline the eyebrow with outline stitch using a single strand of 433.

24. To the left of the eye is a small feather shape that should be filled with freestyle embroidery, using a single strand of 4516. Start in the narrow area closest to the eye with single-weaving shading. When the area widens sufficiently, work a few eye stitches and, perhaps, a three-petal lazy daisy bud, then work single-weaving shading at the end of the shape and add a few filler French knots. *Outline with whipped backstitch using two strands of 498.

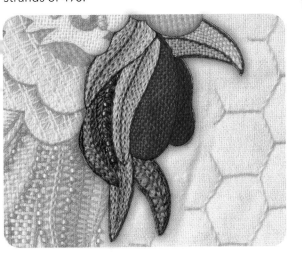

25. Starting with the top left feather and the one just to the right of it, work a row of chain stitch down the centre using two strands of 436. Following the guidelines for chain stitch/ backstitch combination (see page 32), work a line of backstitch down the centre of the chain stitch using two strands of 434. Now work a chain stitch line on either side of the centre line using two strands of 437. Work back-stitches into those lines using two strands of 436. Continue in this way using the following combinations of stranded cotton until you have filled the feather: 738/436, 739/738 and Ecru/739. If you have not filled either of the feathers, add an additional row of the Ecru/739 combination. *Outline the visible edges of the feathers with outline stitch using a single strand of 433.

26. Continuing at the top, fill both of the red wattles with single-weaving shading (see page 44), worked with single strands. Use 3831 for the larger wattle on the left and 498 for the one on the right. *Outline the visible edges of each wattle with outline stitch using a single strand of 498.

27. Moving to the middle row of feathers and starting on the left, the first one is filled with chain stitch – interlaced variation 1 (see page 34); use two strands of 3760 for the chain and side straight

stitches and two strands of 3849 for the interlacing. *Outline the visible edges with whipped back-stitch using two strands of 3765.

28. The little feather squashed in between the one you have just done and the next one is filled with beaded wheatear stitch with variation (see page 53). The wheatear stitch is worked with two strands of 434, the bead is 15° 2422F, the straight stitches on the side are worked with 437 and you should sneak in an additional sliver of a straight stitch above the existing straight stitch using Madeira 3229.

29. Moving to the bottom row of feathers, the one on the left is worked in the same way as those described in step 25 using the following thread combinations: the centre row is 435/434, the rows on either side of the centre are 436/435, the remaining rows are 437/436. *Outline the visible edges with outline stitch using a single strand of 433.

30. The remaining feather is filled with chain stitch – interlaced variation 1 (see page 34); use two strands of 3760 for the chain and side straight-stitches and two strands of 3851 for the interlacing. *Outline the visible edges with whipped back-stitch using two strands of 3765.

31. Each section of the beak is filled with basic double-weaving (see page 64). In the bottom half of the beak, use Dentelles #80 437 for both the warp and the weft stitches. In the top half, use Dentelles #80 Ecru for the warp stitches #80 437 for the wefts. Outline each section of the beak with outline stitch using a single strand of 434.

32. Continuing around the head and starting on the right, fill the first section of the cockscomb with trellis with cross-stitch couching variation 1, using a single strand of 3831. It needs to be closely worked so that it creates a solid-looking, textured fill. *Outline the shape with whipped backstitch using two strands of 3831.

33. Moving left, fill the next section of the cockscomb with vertical long and short stitch shading using a single strand of thread. Start at the base using 498 shading through 3831 to 3832 at the tip. With two strands of 498 and working from tip to base, work loop stitch over the long and short stitch shading. Adjust the tension so that the middle line goes down the centre of the shape. *Outline the visible edges with whipped backstitch using two strands of the same thread.

34. The next section to the left is filled with free-style embroidery as directed in step 1 (see page 87), using a single strand of 4516. *Outline the visible edges with whipped backstitch using two strands of 498.

35. Fill the next section with three rows of chain stitch – interlaced variation 3 (see page 34). Using two strands throughout, the chain stitch and side straight stitches in the middle row are worked with 3832 and interlaced with 3831. For the rows on either side, work the chain stitch and outer edge side-stitches with 3831 and interlace with 498. *Outline the visible edges with whipped back-stitch using two strands of 498.

36. For the next section to the left, repeat step 34.

37. The skinny feather to the left of that is filled with beaded fly-stitch with variation. Use two strands of 3760 and bead 15° 2425 for the beaded fly-stitch and two strands of 3849 for the diagonal straight-stitches. Sneak in an additional diagonal sliver of a straight stitch above the existing straight stitch using Madeira 3037.

38. Fill the next feather with chain stitch - interlaced variation 1 (see page 34), using two strands of 517 for the chain and side straight stitches and two strands of 3851 for the interlacing. *Outline the visible edges with whipped backstitch using two strands of 3760.

39. Coming around the corner of the head, the feather below the two you have just done is filled with chain stitch/backstitch combination as instructed in step 25 (see page 91). The centre row is 435/434, the rows on either side of the centre are 436/435, the rows on either side of those are 437/436 and the remaining rows are 738/437. *Outline the visible edges with outline stitch using a single strand of 433.

40. The feather below that is also worked as instructed in step 25.

41. The curved bead-line that comes out from between the feathers you have just done is worked with beaded backstitch using a doubled-over strand of 407 and bead 15° 641. Work the bead line within the cockscomb in the same way with thread 839 and bead 15° 4249.

42. Now back into the body of the bird, the golden coloured background highlighted in the image above, on the right and curving around the bottom to the left, is filled with trellis couching – cross stitch couching variation 1 shaded (see page 46). Use a single strand each of 436, 437 and 738. Start with the darker, 436, in the uppermost corner slowly changing to 437 as you go around the bend to the lower area. When working the cross stitches, work the uppermost corner as well as the peaks and valleys that go into each point using 436. In the middle area of the top section and the upper half of the bottom section, work the cross stitches with 437. Work the cross stitches of the bottom half of the bottom section with 738. *Outline each side of the bottom section with beaded backstitch using a doubled-over strand of 434 and bead 15° 2422F.

43. Fill the feather at the top left side of the highlighted area in the image with needle-weaving texture no. 2 (see page 67). Use Finca perle #12 8026 for colour 1, the warp stitches, working these over the shortest side. Work the weft stitches in DMC perle #12 437 over the length of the feather. *Outline with whipped backstitch using the perle #12 8026.

44. Fill the two larger feathers that lie between the areas you have just done with chain stitch – interlaced variation 1 (see page 34). When working the bottom feather use two strands of 738 for the chain stitch and side straight stitches. Use two strands of 407 for the interlacing. For the top feather, use 437 for the chain and straight stitches and 3772 for the interlacing. *Outline both feathers with whipped backstitch using two strands of 632.

45. The feathery lines in between the feathers you have just worked are done with a chain stitch/backstitch combination on each of the lines. All of the backstitches are worked with a single strand of S943. Working from the top, above the feather, the chain stitch is worked using two strands of 3851 followed by 3760 and 3849. Between the two feathers, working down with two strands, use 3851 followed by 3847 for the chain stitch. In the final gap, use 3851 and 3760 to work the chain stitch. Work the extra, wispy lines with outline stitch using a single strand of 3847. The feathery lines at the very bottom will be described later (see step 55, page 95).

46. Working with the shape on the top left first, pad each of the semi-circles with horizontal satin stitch using two strands of stranded cotton Ecru. With a single strand of the same thread, work vertical satin stitch over the padding. Using two strands of 738, work three to five detached-chain petals that radiate out and up from the dots depicted between the semi-circles. Using a doubled-over strand of 842, stitch a bead 15° 4249 onto each of the dots. Using a single strand of S943, couch a straight line from the dot down to the bottom between the semi-circles and with the same thread, make a small detached-chain leaf on either side of the flower that you have created around the bead. Work the top border of the shape with beaded knotted cable-chain stitch (see page 53) using two strands of 632. With a doubled-over strand of the same thread, stitch bead 11° 579 into the centre of each of the loops in the stitch line. As you go along attaching the beads, work a French knot with the same thread between each pair of yellow flowers, above the satin-stitched semi-circles. Couch a line of Madeira 3229 on either side of the cable-chain line.

47. Fill the feather at the base of the area you have just worked with chain stitch – interlaced variation 1 using two strands of 842 for the chain and side straight-stitches with two strands of 407 for the interlacing. *Outline with whipped backstitch using two strands of 632.

48. The small feather shape that lies just above the feather you have just done is filled with fly stitch variation using two strands of 3849 for the fly stitch and 3848 for the straight stitches. *Outline the feather with outline stitch using a single strand of 3847.

49. Moving right to the purple flowers, fill the centres with needle-weaving checks and stripes no. 13 (see page 66) using two strands of 3836 for colour 1, the warp stitches. Use two strands each of 3835 for colour 2 and stranded cotton Ecru for colour 3 when working the weft stitches. Fill the outside petal shape with long and short stitch shading using a single strand of 3835 at the base, shading to 3836 on the outer edge. Fill the remaining curved area with three rows of reverse chain stitch. Start at the bottom using two strands of 3835, followed by a row done with two strands of 3836 and finally a row worked with two strands of Ecru. *Outline the visible edges of the petals and the outer edge of the flower centre with outline stitch using a single strand of 3834. Using the same thread, work outline stitch on the outside of the Ecru chain stitch and also in the ditch between the checks and the bottom row of chain stitch.

50. Fill the leaf that comes out of the smaller purple flower with long and short stitch shading with each side of the leaf worked diagonally into the vein. Starting close to the vein, use a single strand of 3848 shading out to 3849. With a single strand of 3847, work outline stitch down the vein and add a few diagonal straight stitches to depict side veins. *With a single strand of 3847, outline the visible edges with outline stitch.

51. Moving to the lower right shape, pad each of the semi-circles with horizontal satin stitch using two strands of stranded cotton Ecru. With a single strand of the same thread, work vertical satin stitch

over the padding. Work three double detached-chain petals that radiate out and down from the dots depicted at the edge of this shape. Use two strands of 3712 for the inner detached chain and two strands of 760 for the outside stitch. Using a doubled-over strand of 842, stitch a bead 15° 4249 onto each of the dots. Using a single strand of S943, work a straight stitch between each pair of petals. *Outline the visible edge of this shape with whipped backstitch using two strands of 632.

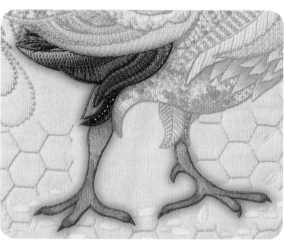

52. Now moving to the area below the shaded trellis with cross stitch couching and starting with the top right feather highlighted in the image above, follow the guidelines for chain stitch – interlaced variation 3 (see page 34). There are three vertical rows. Using two strands throughout, the chain stitch and side stitches in the middle row are worked with 3772 and interlaced with 632. For the rows on either side, work the chain stitch and outer side-stitches with 3772 and interlace those with 407. *Outline the visible edges with whipped backstitch using two strands of 632.

53. Moving left, fill the next feather with buttonhole stitch – up and down, double (see page 31). Working the row that constitutes the upper edge of the feather, use two strands of 3760. Fill in with the second row using a single strand of S943. *Outline the bottom edge, below the ridge of the second row of up and down buttonhole stitch, with outline stitch using a single strand of 3760.

54. Moving further left, fill the next shape with long lines of layered buttonhole stitch. Start with two shorter rows in the upper left corner using two strands of 543. Thereafter work two rows each along the length of the shape using 407, 3772 and 632. Work the last row, to the extent that you can, as an outline row as described in the embroidery stitch gallery (see page 31) using two strands of 632. When you are working adjacent to the previous feather and cannot accommodate the ridge of the buttonhole stitch, fill in the gaps with straight stitches. *Outline the visible edge with outline stitch using a single strand of 839.

55. You are now able to work the remaining feathery lines mentioned in step 45. From the left, work a chain stitch backstitch/combination using 3765/S943, 3851/S943 and 3765/S943. Referring to the colour image before as your guide, add a few wispy lines of outline stitch using a single strand of 3847. One or two of them coming out of the lowest feathery line will be stitched over the layered buttonhole stitch worked in the previous feather.

56. Moving down to the pair of feathers above the left leg, fill the small feather on the left with long and short stitch shading starting at the base with a single strand of 437 shading through 738 to 739 at the tip. *Outline the visible edges with outline stitch using a single strand of 434. The feather next to it should be worked as instructed in step 3 (see page 87).

57. And now to the legs and feet, which you will fill with long and short stitch shading. Referring to the colour image before and working with a single strand throughout, start at the top of the leg with 758 shading down through 738, 739, back to 738 and into 437 at the narrow part of the leg. At the point where the leg splits into the three toes of the feet, shade with 738 in the centre, continuing down into the middle toe then shading through 738 and 754 to 758 at the bottom. For the side toes, continue the shading down with 437 for a while, then shade through 738 and 754 to 758 at the end of the toes. Stitch each claw with a few straight stitches, like satin stitch, using a single strand of 3778. With

the same thread, outline the outside edge of the leg and feet with outline stitch.

58. Starting with the pink flower, fill the centres of each of the petals with woven trellis couching. Using two threads throughout, use 760 for shade 1, 3712 for shade 2 and 761 for shades 3 and 4. Fill the curved area above and adjacent to the centre of the petals with rows of reverse chain stitch. Starting at the base of the arch, aim for about four rows (and in some instances half rows) spreading the colours evenly, using 3712, 760 and 761. Fill the three remaining curved areas at the base of the outside petals with layered buttonhole stitch. Working with two strands throughout, the first row at the base of each area is done with 3848. Follow this with a single row worked with 3849 and finish off with the row that forms the top edge outline using 3847. *Outline the top and bottom of the chain-stitched areas with outline stitch using a single strand of 3328.

59. Moving outwards, fill the area that lies outside the three petals on the left with trellis with cross-stitch couching using a single strand of 842.

60. The leaf that curves around the area you have just done is filled with diagonal long and short stitch shading. Starting adjacent to the spine that curves around the upper edge and shading outwards, use a single strand 437 shading out to 407 and *outlining the outside edge with outline stitch using a single strand of 632.

61. Towards the bottom of and outside the leaf you have just done is a smaller leaf shape. Fill this with needle-weaving checks and stripes no. 13 (see page 66). Colour 1, the warp stitches, should be worked over the shortest side with the weft stitches worked along the length of the feather using DMC perle #12 842 for colour 1, the warp stitches. When working the weft stitches use Finca perle #12 8080 for colour 2 and Finca perle #12 8026 for colour 3. *Outline the visible bottom edges with whipped backstitch using two strands of 839.

62. Now return to the parallel lines that are the vein of the shaded curved leaf. Work knotted cable-chain stitch using two strands of 632 up the line. With a doubled-over strand of the same thread, stitch bead 11° 579 into the centre of each of the loops in the stitch line. Couch a line of Madeira 3229 on either side of the stitched line.

63. Fill the upward facing feather on the right of the pink flower with needle-weaving texture no. 2 – variation (see page 67). Use Finca perle #12 8026 for colour 1, the warp stitches, working these over the shortest side. The weft stitches are worked over the longest side. Use DMC perle #12 437 for colour 2 and DMC perle #12 Ecru for colour 3. *Outline with whipped backstitch using the perle #12 8026.

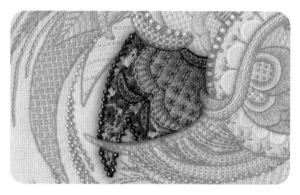

64. Moving down, fill the bottom area with free-style embroidery stitching as instructed in step 1 (see page 87) using a single strand of 4516. *Outline with beaded backstitch using a doubled-over strand of 839 and bead 15° 4249.

65. The small feather shapes that lie within the freestyle embroidered area are filled with fly-stitch variation using two strands of 3849 for the fly stitch and 3848 for the straight stitches. *Outline the feather with outline stitch using a single strand of 3847.

66. Fill the main area of the Jacobean shape with long and short stitch shading using a single strand of thread. Start at the base with 758 shading up to 754. Work trellis couching with cross-stitch filling over the shading using a single strand of 758 for the trellis and a single strand of 3778 for the straight stitches that make up the crosses. The decorative edge outside the main area is double up and down buttonhole stitch (see page 31). Use two strands of 758 for the row that has the purl edge adjacent to the shading and two strands of 754 for the row that has the purl edge adjacent to the freestyle embroidered area. *Outline the outer edge of both purl edges with outline stitch using a single strand of 3778.

67. Moving to the area above the one you have just worked, fill the checked areas of the purple flower with needle-weaving checks and stripes no. 13 (see page 66) using two strands of 3836 for colour 1, the warp stitches. Use two strands each of 3835 for colour 2 and DMC perle #12 Ecru for colour 3 when working the weft stitches. Fill the curved area in between the checks with three

rows of reverse chain stitch. Start adjacent to the smallest checked area using two strands of 3835, followed by a row done with two strands of 3836 and finally a row worked with two strands of Ecru. Using a single strand of 3834, work outline stitch on the outside of the Ecru chain stitch and also in the ditch between the checks and the bottom row of chain stitch. The decorative edge outside the check area is double up and down buttonhole stitch. Use two strands of 3835 for the row that has the purl edge adjacent to the checks and two strands of Ecru for the row that has the purl edge facing outwards. *Outline the outer edge of both purl edges with outline stitch using a single strand of 3834.

68. Fill the feather at the top left of the highlighted area in the image before with chain stitch – interlaced variation 1 (see page 34). Use two strands of 3760 for the chain stitch and side straight-stitches. Use two strands of 3849 for the interlacing and *outline the feather with whipped backstitch using two strands of 3765.

69. Moving right, fill the next feather with long and short stitch shading. Using a single strand, start at the base of the feather with 3772 shading through 407 to 543 at the tip. With a single strand of 632, work fly stitch over the shading, starting at the tip and working down to the base. *Outline the feather with outline stitch using a single strand of the same thread.

70. Moving further right, this feather is identical to the one described in step 68.

71. The final feather in the highlighted area of the image above is identical to the one described in step 7 (see page 88).

72. Fill the main area of the pink motif in the section as highlighted in the image above with long and short stitch shading using a single strand of thread. Start at the base with 3712 shading up to 760. Work trellis couching with cross-stitch filling over the shading using a single strand of 3712 for the trellis and a single strand of 3328 for the straight stitches that make up the crosses. The decorative edge outside the main area is double up and down buttonhole stitch. Use two strands of 3712 for the row that has the purl edge adjacent to the shading and two strands of 760 for the row that has the purl edge facing outwards. *Outline the outer edge of both purl edges with outline stitch using a single strand of 3328.

73. Fill the main part of the feather on the bottom left of the pink motif with raised chain stitch – woven (see page 43). Use two strands of 407 for the raised chain stitches. Twist a length of 632 thread (see Working with twisted thread, page 50) and use this cord to weave over and under the threads that run between the raised-chain knot. *Outline the visible edges with whipped backstitch using two strands of 632, working a double row on the upper side. Using a doubled-over single strand of 842 stitch evenly spaced single beads 15° 641 between the double lines.

74. Moving clockwise around the pink motif and using identical threads and beads, fill the next small feather following the instructions set out in step 6 (see page 88). *Outline the visible edges of this feather with outline stitch using a single strand of 437.

75. Still moving clockwise around the pink motif, fill the next feather with woven trellis couching. Working with two strands throughout, use 437 for shade 1 and 739 for shade 2. For shades 3 and 4, use 407. *Outline with beaded backstitch using a doubled-over strand of 434 and bead 15° 2422F.

76. Moving to the bottom motif on the right of the pink motif, work horizontal satin stitch padding in the semi-circle at the base using two strands of DMC perle #12 Ecru. With a single strand of the same thread, work vertical satin stitch over the padding. Moving up, fill the main area with long and short stitch shading worked with a single strand. Start at the base with 3778 shading through 758 to 754 at the top. Work basic trellis couching over the shading with a single strand of 3778. The decorative edge above the main area is double up and down buttonhole stitch. Use two strands of 758 for the row that has the purl edge adjacent to the shading and two strands of 754 for the row that has the purl edge at the top. *Outline the outer edge of both purl edges with outline stitch using a single strand of 3778.

77. The feather above and to the right of the motif you have just done is worked with interlaced chain stitch variation 1 (see page 34). Use two strands of 632 for the chain stitch and side straight-stitches. Use two strands of 407 for the interlacing and *outline the visible edges with whipped backstitch using two strands of 632.

78. Pad the semi-circles in the motif to the left with horizontal satin stitch using two strands of DMC perle #12 Ecru. With a single strand of the same thread, work vertical satin stitch over the padding. Using two strands of 3835, work three detached-chain petals that radiate out and up from the dots depicted between the semi-circles. Using a doubled-over strand of 842, stitch a bead 15°

4249 onto each of the dots. Using a single strand of S943, place a French knot below each bead and, at the same time, work a small straight leaf on either side of the flower that you have created around the bead. With two strands of 739, place a French knot in the middle of the space above the semi-circles. *Work whipped backstitch, using two strands of 632, on all the lines that form the single and double outlines of this feather. With a doubled-over strand of the same thread, stitch beads 15° 641 evenly spaced between the double outlines on the left.

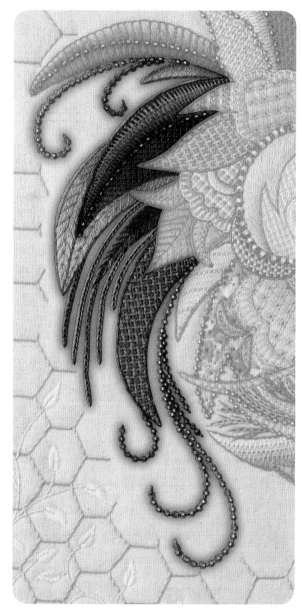

79. And now to the tail feathers. Starting with the small terracotta feather at the top of the highlighted area in the image on page 98, work diagonal long and short stitch shading using a single strand of thread. Use 758 from tip to base on the lower side, shading up to 3778 on the upper side. *Outline the visible edges with outline stitch using a single strand of 3830.

80. Moving down, work each side of the second terracotta feather separately with long and short stitch shading using a single strand of thread. Start at the base with 3778 shading through 758 to 754 at the tips. With a single strand of 3778, work fly stitch over the long and short stitch shading on each side. *Outline the edges and work down the vein with outline stitch using a single strand of 3830.

81. Now work the feather that goes into the feather you have just done. Fill the lower half with long and short stitch shading that starts at the base with a single strand of 311. Work vertically up the feather shading through 3842 to 3760 at the tip. With a single strand of 3847, work basic trellis couching over the shading and *outline the bottom edge with outline stitch using the same thread.

82. The top of half this feather is filled with layered buttonhole stitch. Using two strands throughout, start adjacent to the vein with a row done with 3842. Follow that with single rows worked with 3765, 3848, 3851 and finally, the close outline row worked with 3847. Work beaded backstitch up the vein using a doubled-over strand of 3847 and bead 15° 2425.

83. The small feather below the large terracotta feather is filled with long and short stitch shading. Using a single strand throughout and working vertically from base to tip, start with 3847 shading through 517, 3760 and 3848 to 3851 at the tip. With a single strand of 3847, work fly stitch over the shading from tip to base.

84. Work the feathery lines with a chain stitch/backstitch combination as described in step 45 (see page 93), using the following threads, from the top line: 3765/S943; 3851/S943; 3760/S943;

3849/S943 and 3851/S943 at the bottom.

85. Moving down, fill the lowest feather highlighted in the image on page 98 with woven trellis couching using two strands of cotton as follows: Shade 1 is 3760; shade 2 is 517; shades 3 and 4 are 3851. *Outline the visible edges with whipped backstitch using two strands of 517.

86. All of the remaining tendril-like feathers in the image are worked with beaded backstitch using, from the top, the following doubled-over single strand thread and bead combinations. Coming out above the feather described in step 79: 407/15° 641; 632/15° 4249. Coming off the lower half of the feather described in step 85: 632/15° 4249. Starting just below the top of the feather described in step 85, including the shorter tendril that goes off on the right about halfway down: 632/15° 4249. Coming out on the left are two curls. The one on the left is worked with 632/15° 641 and the longest one to the right of that is worked with 407/15° 641.

87. Moving on with the tail feathers, starting on the left, fill each side of this feather with diagonal long and short stitch that starts at the vein shading out to the edge on each side. Working with a single strand, the bottom section uses 3842 shading out to 517. For the top section, start with 3765 shading through 3848 to 3851. With a single strand of 3847, work up and down buttonhole stitch over the shaded areas on both sides. In each instance, the purl edge lies on the outside edge, creating an

outline at the same time. Work beaded backstitch up the vein using a doubled-over strand of 3847 and bead 15° 2425.

88. Fill the left-hand side of the next feather (working clockwise), with layered buttonhole stitch using two strands of thread. Starting against the central vein do single rows of each colour as follows: 3830, 3778, 758, 754, 758, 3778. Work the final row with 3830, close to the purl of the previous row, creating an outline in the process. The bead tendrils that come out of this side of the feather are worked with beaded backstitch. Start at the bottom using a doubled-over strand of 632 and bead 15° 4249. Use 407 and bead 15° 641 for the long line and finally, 632 and bead 15° 4249 for the short line that comes out of the long tendril.

89. The right-hand side of this feather is filled with long and short stitch shading which starts at the base of the feather, shading up to the tip, using single strands of thread in the following order: 3765, 517, 3842, 3760, 3848 and 3851. Work basic trellis couching over the shading with a single

strand of 3847 and, with the same thread *outline the outside edge with outline stitch. Work beaded backstitch up the vein using a doubled-over strand of 3847 and bead 15° 2425.

90. Fill the left-hand side of the next feather (the third working clockwise) with woven trellis couching. Working with two strands throughout use 3778 for shade, 3830 for shade 2 and 754 for shades 3 and 4. *Outline the visible edge with whipped backstitch using two strands of 3830.

91. The right-hand side of this feather is filled with diagonal long and short stitch shading that starts at the vein shading out to the edge using single strands of thread. In the area close to the base of the feather until about the point where the feather forks into two, start with 311. Thereafter, continue with 517 that shades into the darker blue and continues up to the tip. From there shade into 3848 and 3851. With the purl on the outside edge, work up and down buttonhole stitch over the shading with a single strand of 3847. Necessarily, the downward stitch is very long and you should couch it twice from the base to the fork, trying to keep the couching stitches in line with one another. After the fork, couch the stitches only once on each side and with the same thread, *outline the bottom edge of the right fork with outline stitch. Work beaded backstitch up the vein using a doubled-over strand of 3847 and bead 15° 2425.

92. The tendril feathers that come out of the side you have just worked are, like the others, worked with beaded backstitch. Using the above image as your guide, use a doubled-over single thread 632 and bead 15° 4249 for the darker lines. Single thread 407 and bead 15° 641 should be used to work the lighter lines.

93. The left-hand side of the final feather is filled with diagonal long and short stitch that starts at the vein shading out to the edge. Working with a single strand, use 3765 shading through 517, 3760 and 3848 to 3851 on the edge. With a single strand of 3847, work basic trellis couching over the shading and with the same thread, work outline stitch along the visible left-side edges.

94. Work beaded backstitch up the vein of the leaf you have just done using a doubled-over strand of 3847 and bead 15° 2425. Thereafter, working to the right, work beaded backstitch on the third line away from that using thread 632 and bead 15° 4249. On the final line, work beaded backstitch using 407 and bead 15° 641.

95. Now work lines of chain stitch/backstitch combination on the remaining lines, adding one or two extra if you have the space (not all the lines are in the drawing as they would have mingled and messed). Using a single strand of S943 for all of the backstitch and two strands of thread for the chain stitch, I worked from the top using 3760, 3851 and 3847 above the darker beaded backstitch line with a single line of 3760 below it. Fill in some additional wispy lines done with outline stitch using a single strand of 3847.

If you are intending to turn this project into the page of a book as I have done, and you did not add the batting and additional voile backing from the beginning, you should now remove the project from the frame.

Place a layer of voile, then a layer of batting, then the project so far back over the frame and secure it all together, making sure that you stretch all of the layers as you go. There should be no folds visible on the back of the work. Everything should be smooth and well secured.

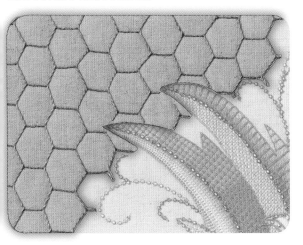

96. The chicken wire is worked through the three layers, or, if you are going to work it as a framed picture, as opposed to quilting it, just the one. Make sure your work is well stretched in the frame to avoid puckering.

Using two strands of 646, work a short diagonal backstitch facing down to the first horizontal line at the top of the project and thereafter, work five similar sized backstitches on that line, ending off with a short diagonal backstitch facing up and out of the line. Repeat this on each of the horizontal lines depicted as the first row in the background to the rooster.

97. Moving down to the second row:

Using the same thread, work five backstitches on the first horizontal line in the second row. Bring the needle up at the end of the row, take the needle under the short diagonal backstitch at the beginning of the backstitch line in the first row. Continue by whipping the five backstitches, going under the short diagonal backstitch at the end of the backstitch line and go into the fabric at the beginning of the next line in the second row. Continue working down the second row to the other end.

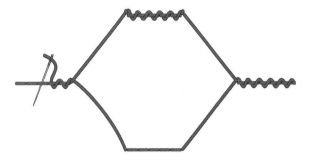

99. Turn your work on its side and with two strands of 648, whip each of the long strands that lie diagonally between the rows. Always start from the same side and work continuously from top to bottom. Whipping each long strand five times, take the needle into the fabric at the bottom and end off.

98. Work the third and all subsequent rows in the same way, always starting on the same side of the project, still using two strands of 646, and referring to the illustration above. Start by whipping the five backstitches of the previous row. After you have whipped the last stitch, go under the thread that went up towards the row before that – the one used to whip those backstitches – and go into the fabric at the beginning of the next line in the work, making five backstitches. Continue working down the row to the other end. When you get to the very last row, the five-backstitch sets in that row will be unwhipped. Come up at the beginning of each set and whip the five stitches, going in at the end of each set.

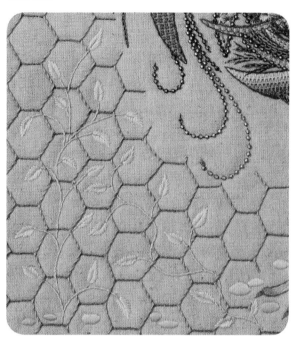

100. All of the stems of the creepers that weave in and out of the chicken wire are worked with whipped backstitch using two strands of 842. Work all of the leaves with two strands of 543 following the guidelines for satin-stitch leaf (see page 44).

101. To work the pebbles that are scattered on the ground at the base of the creepers, work split backstitch on the line that depicts the outline of each petal. With a single strand of the same thread, work vertical satin stitch over the pebble. Referring to those highlighted in the image above and working from the left, use the following threads: 842, 648, 842, 648, 842.

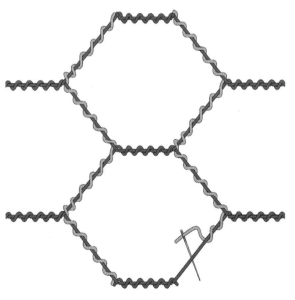

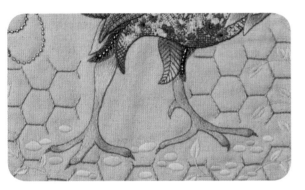

102. To stitch the pebbles highlighted in the image above, work from the left using the following threads: 842, 543, 842 (top), 648 (bottom between the two claws), 842, 648, 842, at the top 648, 543, at the bottom 543, 658, the group of three is 648, 842 at the top and 543 at the bottom. Working the next groups, starting with the bottom five, use 648. 543, 842, 852 and 648. The top four pebbles from the left are 543, 648, 842 and 543.

103. Work the creepers on the right of the bird as described in step 100. The pebbles are worked as described in step 101 using 543, 648 and 543 from left to right.

Dave

The common pheasant, whilst not the brightest of the species, combines colours that are challenging but were too tempting to resist. This project measures 310 x 280 mm (12¼ x 11").

Materials

Farbric

450 x 450 mm (18 x 18") medium-weight linen-cotton blend base fabric, colour Natural

450 x 450 mm (18 x 18") off-white cotton-voile backing fabric x 2

450 x 450 mm (18 x 18") 100 gsm polyester or cotton batting

Embroidery frame

2 pairs 17″ Edmunds stretcher bars

Needles

Size 7 Embroidery needles
Size 10 Embroidery needles
Size 11 Sharps quilting needles
Size 26 Tapestry needles

Threads and beads

DMC STRANDED COTTON

9	Very Dark Cocoa
309	Dark Rose
311	Medium Navy Blue
315	Medium Dark Antique Mauve
407	Dark Desert Sand
436	Tan
498	Dark Red
517	Dark Wedgewood
632	Ultra Very Dark Desert Sand
640	Very Dark Beige Grey
642	Dark Beige Grey
644	Medium Beige Grey
647	Medium Beaver Grey
779	Dark Cocoa
943	Medium Aquamarine
975	Dark Golden Brown
976	Medium Golden Brown
3033	Very Light Mocha Brown
3772	Very Dark Desert Sand
3726	Dark Antique Mauve
3760	Medium Wedgewood
3781	Dark Mocha Brown
3782	Light Mocha Brown
3790	Ultra Dark Beige Grey
3802	Very Dark Antique Mauve
3842	Dark Wedgwood
3847	Dark Teal Green
3848	Medium Teal Green
3850	Dark Bright Green
3851	Light Bright Green
3860	Cocoa
3861	Light Cocoa
3865	Winter White

DMC DIAMANT METALLIC THREAD

D316	Medium Antique Mauve
D3821	Light Gold

DMC DENTELLES #80

437	Light Tan
712	Cream

FINCA PERLE #12

4000	Dark Ecru
8026	Dark Taupe

FINCA PERLE #16

7656	Dark Mahogany
7944	Dark Desert Sand
8742	Medium Shell Gray
8756	Almost Black

MADEIRA GLAMOUR #12 METALLIC THREAD

3037	Jade green

MIYUKI BEADS

2g	15° 4243	SL Topaz Gold
2g	15° 4245	SL Nutmeg
2g	15° 4247	SL Peony Pink
2g	15° 4249	SL Rose Bronze

PRECIOSA VIVA 12 FLAT-BACK CRYSTALS

1 piece 20ss Smoke Topaz AB
3 pieces 20ss Emerald AB

General instructions

- Refer to the general project instructions on page 19.

Stitching instructions

*Throughout this design you will be instructed to finish off sections with outlines. This will be done with stitches as described in each section, but you should not work these outlines until all surrounding embroidery has been done.

1. Following the guidelines for single weaving with stranded cotton (see page 45), fill the main part of the beak using two strands of 3033. Work the warp stitches vertically over the short side, weaving horizontally over the long side. Fill the narrow, bottom part of the beak using two strands of 3790 and the top, shorter part using two strands of 3782.

2. With two strands of 3033, pad the semi-circular shape that abuts the head with horizontal satin stitch. With a single strand of the same thread, work vertical satin stitch over the padding.

3. *Outline each section of the beak with outline stitch using a single strand of 3781.

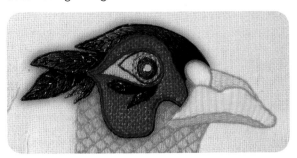

4. Referring to the instructions for single weaving shading (see page 44) and using a single strand of 309, fill the red area around the eye leaving gaps for the small blue feathers under the eye. *Outline the outside edges with whipped backstitch using two strands of 498.

5. Using a single strand of 3842, fill the small blue feathers with long and short stitch shading. Work fly stitch over the long and short stitch shading, from tip to base, using Madeira 3037.

6. Referring to the instructions for caging a flat-back crystal (see page 53), attach a 20ss smoked topaz crystal to the circle in the middle of the eye using a single strand of 3781. Using two strands of 436, work rows of split backstitch around the caged crystal to complete the larger circle. With two strands of 3781, work split backstitch on the eye-shaped line within the larger eye shape. Start at the point on the left, work around the tan split-backstitched circle, continuing back to the point. Finally, *outline the line of the larger eye shape with whipped backstitch using two strands of 498.

7. Moving to the area above and around the eye area, fill the top of the head and plumage with long and short stitch shading. Using single strands of thread and starting against the base of the beak, work with 311 shading through 3842, 3847, 3848 and back to 3847 in the tip of the feather at the back of the head. The feather below that uses 3842 at the base shading through 3847 to 3848 at the tip. The next feather uses 311 at the base shading out to 3847. The small feather below that starts at the base with 3847 shading out to 3848 and the small feather at the bottom uses 3847 only. Referring to the colour image on the left and using Madeira 3037, work fly stitch over the shading of the feathers. *Outline the top of the head and the two larger feathers with outline stitch using a single strand of 311.

to outline the bottom of the scallops. *Outline the lower edge of the bottom row of scallops in the same way.

10. Fill each of the white feathers below the neck scallops with fly stitch using two strands of 3865.

8. Moving to the neck of the bird, start with the lower line of scallops. Using two strands of 3851, work split backstitch on the outside curve of each scallop. Using a single strand of the same thread, work long and short buttonhole, starting on the outside of the split backstitch and working into the shape. With a single strand of 943, shade from within the long and short buttonhole with long and short stitch, finishing at the base of the shape. Do the same for the extra scallop that lies between the first and second lines of scallops on the right of the neck.

9. Moving to the upper line of scallops, using two strands of 943, work split backstitch on the outside curve of each scallop. Using a single strand of the same thread, work long and short buttonhole, starting on the outside of the split backstitch and working up the neck. Thereafter, work long and short stitch shading into the long and short buttonhole, continuing up to the red patch around the eye. Using single strands, start with 3760 shading through 517 and 3842 to 311 in the nooks and crannies at the top of the neck. Using a single strand of 311 and referring to the colour image above, work intermittent trellis couching in the blue areas of the neck. With the same thread, work outline stitch on each of the outside edges of the blue area changing to a single strand of 3850

11. The ruffle of feathers below the neck is filled with long and short stitch shading. Using a single strand throughout, start adjacent to the white feathers at the bottom of the neck with 779 shading through 3860 and 315 to 3726 at the tips. When you have completed the shading and referring to the image above, work feather-like lines of fly stitch over the shaded area. Using a single strand and without working over the light tips, work with 315 over approximately the bottom third and 3726 over about a third in the middle of the shading. *Outline the ruffle with outline stitch using a single strand of 315.

12. The two areas below the ruffle are worked in the same way. Fill the centre of each area with woven trellis couching (see page 47). Using two strands throughout, work shade 1 with 3772. Shade 2 is worked with 632 and the weaving stitches of shades 3 and 4 are worked with 407.

13. Work striped blanket stitch over the scalloped edge. With the purl edge on the outside, use Finca perle #12 8026 for the blanket stitch. Work a straight stitch in the middle of each space with Diamant D316. With a single strand of 315, do a straight stitch on either side of the metallic thread stitch. Work a scalloped line of beaded backstitch in the ditch below the striped blanket stitch using a doubled-over strand of 315 and bead 15° 4247. *Outline the scalloped shape with outline stitch on the outside of the purl edge using a single strand of 315.

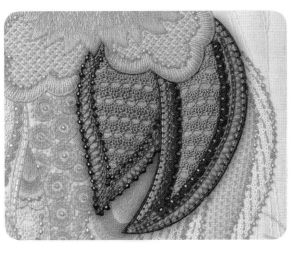

14. Moving into the body of the bird and starting with the feather shape on the left, outline the middle with backstitch using Finca perle #16 7944. Using the same thread work needle-lace stitch no. 10 (see page 57) over the middle area using the backstitch to anchor the needle-lace stitches at the top and on the sides. *Outline the needle-laced area with beaded backstitch, working over the backstitches that secure the needle lace. Use a doubled-over strand of 632 and bead 15° 4245.

15. Using two strands of 3726 and following the guidelines for interlaced chain-stitch – variation 2 (see page 34), work chain stitch on the two lines that merge at the bottom of the feather with their related side stitches on the outside lines of the shape. Work the interlacing with Fina perle #12 8026. *Outline the visible edges of the feather with beaded backstitch using a doubled-over strand of 315 and bead 15° 4247.

16. Moving to the feather on the right in the image above, outline the middle with backstitch using Dentelles #80 437. Using the same thread work needle-lace stitch no. 10 over the middle area using the backstitch to anchor the needle-lace stitches at the top and on the sides.

17. To create the scalloped edge around the needle-laced area:

- Start by marking small dots adjacent to the two lines that form the visible side edges of the needle lace. Do this with a Pilot Frixion heat erasable pen and place the dots 4 mm (approximately ⅛") apart. Going past the pointed tip, mark an additional dot.
- Starting at the top (which is the base of the feather) and using Finca perle #16 7656 , come up on the first dot. Going in on the second dot, work a cast-on buttonhole bar (see page 32) that has 10 cast-on loops. The stitch, when completed, should form a scallop and you might find you need to do either more or fewer cast on stitches. Everyone works with a different tension.
- Working through the backstitches around the needle-laced area, come up halfway up the gap between the beginning and the end of the buttonhole bar. Work a backstitch into the hole where you started the buttonhole bar. Come up through the hole where you ended the buttonhole bar and work a backstitch that goes into the beginning of the first backstitch.
- Come up through the hole where you started the second backstitch and create the next cast on buttonhole bar, taking it down through the next marked dot on the line.
- Keep working down the line in the same way to the tip, working the last bar utilising the additional dot that you marked out. Do not work additional backstitches when you have worked this bar.
- Work the opposite edge of the needle-laced area in the same way. The last bar, with no backstitches, will be worked out of and into the same holes as the last bar on the other side, creating something akin to an oval shape.
- It is unlikely that these looped buttonhole bars will lie flat so, to force them into the position that you would like, thread a doubled-over strand of 975 onto a bead embroidery needle. Starting at the top of one of the lines work down

doing a small couching stitch between the fifth and sixth cast-on stitches of the buttonhole bar to secure it in the correct position. Before moving on, stitch a bead 15° 4243 inside the looped bullion bar and in the oval-shaped gap between the buttonhole bars at the tip.

• Using two strands of 976, work a French knot in the valleys adjacent to where the looped buttonhole bars meet. Work four single-wrap French knots beyond the tip thereby filling what would otherwise be a bit of a gaping hole once you have completed the next step.

18. Using two strands of 975 and following the guidelines for interlaced chain-stitch – variation 2 (see page 34), work chain stitch on the two lines that merge at the bottom of the feather with their related side stitches on the outside lines of the shape. Work the interlacing with two strands of 436. *Outline the visible edges of the feather with whipped backstitch using Finca perle #16 7656 . Using Diamant D3821 and coming up through the fabric adjacent to the striped blanket stitch described in step 13 above, thread under each of the rust brown side-stitches that are part of the interlaced chain-stitch. Go into the fabric at the bottom, end off and do the same on the other side.

19. Moving now to the left of where you have been working and starting with the feather on the right, work concentric circles of chain stitch in the circles depicted. Using single strands of thread throughout, start just outside the inner circle working a circle with 3802. Work a circle with 315 outside that one and, a circle with 3726 to bring you to the edge of the last circle. Outline each circle with outline stitch using a single strand of 3802. Using a single strand of 407, work a buttonhole circle in the middle of all the circles, completing it by stitching a bead 15° 4245 in the centre. *Outline the visible edges of this feather with whipped backstitch using two strands of 3802.

20. Moving to the left, this feather is worked in the same way as the one described in steps 16 to 18 before.

21. Moving to the middle of the next feather on the left:

• Work the middle with needle-lace stitch no. 10 (see page 57) using Dentelles #80 437.

• Outline the needle-laced area with beaded knotted cable-chain stitch (see page 53) using Finca perle #16 7656 and bead 15° 4243.

• Using the same thread and referring to the guidelines for interlaced backstitch (see page 26), work backstitch down the lines in the middle of the edge of this feather, with the side stitches being placed on the outside lines. Use two strands of 976 for the interlacing.

• Using the same thread, work French knots in the valleys adjacent to where the knotted cable-chain stitches meet. Work three French knots beyond the tip of the cable-chain outline thereby filling what would otherwise be a bit of a gaping hole between that outline and the interlaced backstitch.

• *Outline the visible edges of this feather with whipped backstitch using Finca perle #16 7656.

22. Moving down to the next row of feathers in the body and starting in the centre, work both of these feathers in the same way as follows:

- Fill the base of the feather with long and short stitch shading. Using single strands of thread and starting where it comes out from underneath the row above use 311 shading through 3842, 517 and 3847 to 3848 at the curved edge. Work one row of each shade in the feather on the left and two rows of each shade in the one on the right.
- The curved area adjacent to the shading is done with rows of chain stitch using two strands of thread. Start with 779 and moving through 3860 to 3861. Use the image above to guide you in dividing the colours.
- Before working the curved edges adjacent to the chain stitch, work the lower part of the feather following the guidelines set out in steps 14 and 15 (see page 109).
- Return to the curved borders outside the chain-stitched area and fill each one with striped blanket stitch as set out in step 13 (see page 108).

23. Moving to the feather on the far-right:

- Fill the centre with needle-weaving texture no. 3 (see page 68) using Finca perle #16 7944 for colour 1 and 7656 for colour 2.
- Moving onto the edge of this feather and using Dentelles #80 712, work backstitch around the woven area, around the outside lines on either side and, also, along the line that runs from the tip of the weaving to the tip of the feather.
- Using the same thread, fill each side separately with needle-lace stitch no. 9 with variation (see page 57). Because you want the woven twisted cord to form lines that would go in the same direction as you would find on a feather, use both the dotted lines in the drawing and also the image above to guide you in the placement of the first row of needle-lace stitches on both sides.

- Twist a single strand (see page 50) of Finca perle #16 7656 and use that to weave over and under the rows to complete the needle-lace stitching.
- Using a doubled-over strand of 632 and bead 15° 4245, work beaded backstitch in the ditch between the weaving and the needle lace. Using the same combination, *outline the visible edge of the feather with beaded backstitch.

24. Moving to the feather on the left, fill this area with needle-lace stitch no. 9 with variation. Using Dentelles #80 437, work backstitch around the shape and work the needle lace with the same thread using both the dotted lines in the drawing and also the image above to guide you in the placement of the first row of needle-lace stitches which is worked from the left side of the shape. Twist a single strand of stranded cotton 9 to weave over and under the rows to complete the needle-lace stitching. *Outline the visible edges of this feather with beaded backstitch using a doubled-over strand of 9 and bead 15° 4249.

25. Work the top feather using the instructions for step 21.

26. Work the bottom feather using the instructions for step 24.

27. Moving to the far left of the pheasant's body:
- Fill the main part at the base of each of these shapes with needle-weaving texture no. 5 – 1 (see page 68). This is best done by turning your work anti-clockwise so that the left side of the project sits in your lap. Work colour 1, the warp stitches over the shortest side with colour 2, the weft stitches being worked along the length of the shape.
- For the shape closest to the body use Dentelles #80 437 for colour 1, the warp stitches and 712 for colour 2, the weft stitches. The smaller shape on the edge of the body uses 437 for both the warp and the weft stitches, giving a darker appearance.
- The curved shapes at the tips of these feathers are filled with striped blanket stitch, working as you did in step 13 (see page 108).
- For the inside, lighter feather, use two strands of 436 for the blanket stitch, Diamant D3821 for the middle stripe and a single strand of 779 for the straight stitch on either side of the middle, shiny stripe. *Work outline stitch on the outside of each purl edge using a single strand of 779.
- To work the two curved shapes at the tip of the darker, outside feather, use two strands of 976 for the blanket stitch, Diamant D3821 for the middle stripe and a single strand of 9 for the straight stitch on either side of the middle, shiny stripe. *Work outline stitch on the outside of each purl edge using a single strand of 9.

- Using a doubled-over strand of 9 and bead 15° 4249, worked beaded backstitch in the ditch between the woven area and the adjacent outer curved shape of both feathers. Continue this around the side of the woven area to complete the outline.

28. Starting from the bottom, fill each of the brown feathers with raised stem stitch. Using two strands of thread, the one on the left is worked with 3772, the middle feather is done with 407 and the one on the right uses 3772. *Outline each feather individually with outline stitch using a single strand of 632.

29. Moving up, work the oval shapes that cascade down towards the brown feathers:

- Following the guidelines for caging a flat-back crystal (see page 53), attach a 20ss flat back crystal, Emerald AB over each of the small circles within the semi-circles using a single strand of 3847.
- Thereafter, work circles and part-circles of chain stitch around the attached crystals using single strands of thread.

- Start adjacent to the crystal with 3847. Follow up using 3760, 517 and 3842. Using the image above as your guide, vary the number of rows for each colour according to each individual oval shape.
- *Outline the visible edge of each oval shape with whipped backstitch using two strands of 311.

30. The feathers that protrude from the oval shapes are worked with long and short stitch shading. Using single strands of thread and working from base to tip, both feathers are worked with 3847 shading through 3842 and 517 to 3760 at the tip. Work fly stitch over the shading with Madeira 3037 and *outline each feather with outline stitch using a single strand of 311.

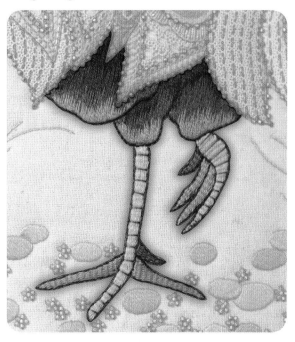

31. Moving to the bottom of the body, fill each of the three sections going down to the legs and feet with long and short stitch shading using the image above as a guideline for the colour distribution. Starting in the area that comes out from under the feathers and working with single strands, use 9 shading through 779 and 3860 to 3861 at the bottom. *Outline the visible edge with outline stitch using a single strand of 9.

32. Fill each section of the legs and feet with single weaving – bird's leg variation (see page 65) using stranded cotton. Work the warp stitch over the short side of each section, with the wefts running along the length as follows.

- Start with the left leg, working all the way down to the toe in the front using two strands of 3033. When you have completed the weaving, using a single strand of 3790, work horizontal straight stitches over the top approximately over where every second warp stitch has been buried.
- Weave the large toes on either side of that leg with 3782 and the small toe on the top right with 3790.
- Outline each section of the leg and toes with outline stitch using a single strand of 3781.
- Moving to the foot on the right, weave the top part of the foot, continuing down the toe in the front with 3790 and work horizontal, fanning straight stitches over the weaving, as you did on the other leg, with 3790.
- Moving up the foot, weave the next two toes with 3782 and the small claw at the top with 3790.
- Outline each section of the foot and toes with outline stitch using a single strand of 3781.

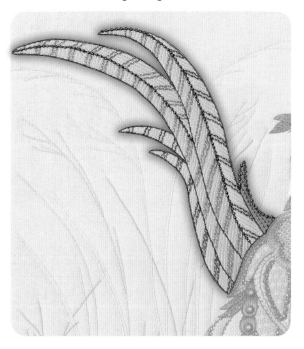

33. Working with the main tail feathers, fill each tail feather with needle-weaving texture no. 5 as follows:

34. Working from the left and starting with the shortest tail feather, turn your work anti-clockwise so that the left side of the design sits in your lap.

- Using Finca perle #12 4000, fill the feather following the guidelines for needle-weaving texture no. 5 – 1 (see page 68) so that the line created by the weft stitches slopes from top left to bottom right.
- Following the directions for double-weaving twill with variation 2 (see page 70), weave the diagonal stripes in this part of the tail using Finca perle #16 8756.
- *Outline the visible edges of the feather with outline stitch using a single strand of 9.
- The small tip of the feather just above this feather is worked in the same way.

35. Moving to the right, turn your work anti-clockwise so that the left side of the design sits in your lap and work the larger feather as follows:

- Using Finca perle #12 4000 fill the left side of the feather following the guidelines for needle-weaving texture no. 5 – 1 so that the line created by the weft stitches slopes from top left to bottom right.
- Using the same thread, fill the right, shorter side of the feather following the guidelines for needle-weaving texture no. 5 – 2 (mirror image) so that the line created by the weft stitches slopes from bottom left to top right.
- Following the directions for double-weaving twill with variation 2, weave the diagonal stripes on both sides of the feather using Finca perle #16 8742 and making sure that they line up where they meet at the vein where it exists.
- Using a doubled-over strand of 9 and bead 15° 4249, work beaded backstitch on the vein from where it starts about halfway up the feather to the tip.
- *Outline the visible edges of the feather with outline stitch using a single strand of 9.

36. Moving right, turn your work anti-clockwise so that the left side of the design sits in your lap and work the largest feather as follows:

- Using Finca perle #12 4000 fill the left side of the feather following the guidelines for needle-weaving texture no. 5 – 1 so that the line created by the weft stitches slopes from top left to bottom right.
- Using the same thread, fill the right, shorter side of the feather following the guidelines for needle-weaving texture no. 5 – 2 (mirror image) so that the line created by the weft stitches slopes from bottom left to top right.
- Following the directions for double-weaving twill with variation 2, weave the diagonal stripes on both sides of the feather using Finca perle #16 8742 on the left and 8756 on the right. Make sure that they line up where they meet at the vein.
- Using a doubled-over strand of 9 and bead 15° 4249, work beaded backstitch on the vein from the base, up the feather to the tip.
- *Outline the visible edges on both sides of the feather with outline stitch using a single strand of 9.

37. The small copper brown feather on the right of this large feather is filled with needle-weaving texture no. 3 (see page 68) using Finca perle #16 7944 for colour 1 and 7656 for colour 2. *Outline the visible edges with beaded backstitch using a doubled-over strand of 632 and bead 15° 4245.

If you are intending to turn this project into the page of a book as I have done, and you did not add the batting and additional voile backing from the beginning, you should now remove the project from the frame.

Place a layer of voile, then a layer of batting, then the project so far, back over the frame and secure it all together, making sure that you stretch all of the layers as you go. There should be no folds visible on the back of the work. Everything should be smooth and well secured.

38. All the grass stems in the background are worked with whipped backstitch in a variety of shades. As would be the nature of grass, they sometimes cross over one another and you should do the same going either under or over existing stems. Starting from the left in the bottom left corner of the project, working towards the bird up until where you reach the area close to the left and feet, identifying each stem where it starts at its base, use two strands of the following threads: all branches 642; both branches 3782; two stems that join at the tip 3033; all branches 3782; two stems that join at the tip 3033; all branches 642; 3033 for the main stem and the stem that branches off to the left about halfway up should be done with 644; 642; 644; two stems that join at the tip after they have gone under the tail feathers 3033; 3782; all branches 642; 644.

39. Moving to the area between the tail feathers and Dave's head, working from top left down the side of the tail feathers to bottom right, identifying each stem where it starts at its base, use two strands of the following threads: 3033; 644; 644; 3033; 642; 3782; 644.

40. Moving to the bottom right area of the project, working from the left away from Dave's body and feet, identifying each stem where it starts at its base. Once you get past the body, the stems will continue to the top of the project. Use two strands of the following threads: 644; 3782; two stems that join at the tip after they have gone behind the body as well as the right-side branch that continues up towards the top 3033; all branches 642. The next one consists of the main branch being worked with 644 to the top. The branch that goes off to the left and then twists right up to the top is worked with 3782 and the one that goes off the right and curves left at the top (reiterated in the next set of instructions) is worked with 3033. The branch on the extreme right is worked with 642.

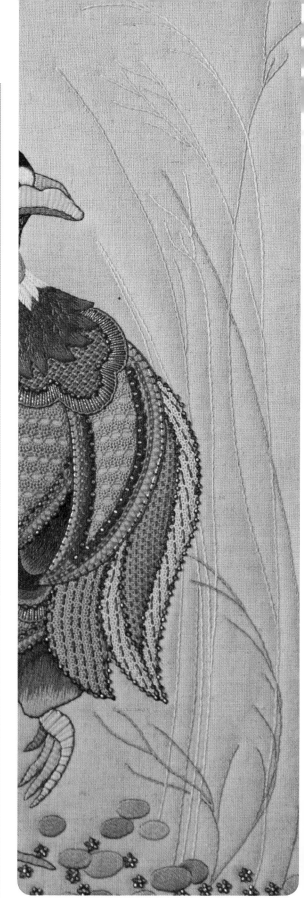

41. All of the stems on the top right of the project are a continuation of stems started at the bottom. Thread colours are repeated here to provide confirmation. Use two strands of thread as follows: two stems that join at the tip 3033; both branches 3782; main stem and side branches at the tip; crossing over is the branch that has come from the far right base 642; the next branch is the one coming from the main stem one in from the extreme right and is worked with 3782; the next one is the main stem which is worked with 644 and the final one is the branch that goes off on the right of that main stem and curves around to the left in a canopy formation, 3033.

42. Moving to the bottom of the project, start by filling the pebbles.

- Using the threads noted, work split backstitch around the circumference or part thereof with two strands of thread. With a single strand of thread, work satin stitch over the pebble starting and ending the stitches on the outside of the split backstitch. Working from the left the colours you should use are as follows: 647; 3790; 640; 647; 642; 3790; 642; 647; 3790; 642; 647; 640; 3790; 642; 647. The three at the top, from the left are 640; 3790 and 647.

- Each of the small circles in the drawing is the centre of a little five-petal bead flower. Using a doubled-over strand of 3782, stitch a bead 15° 4243 on the small circle. Surround the circle with five beads 15° 4247 stitched onto the fabric with the same thread.

43. Moving to the area around the feet, the pebbles and bead flowers are worked in the same way.

- Working along the bottom line of pebbles starting on the left use 3790; 647; 642; 3790 and 647.

- The pebble between the two toes is worked with 640 and the two on the right of the toe are done with 647 and 642.

- Starting on the left of the leg, work with 642. On the right of the leg work with 640; 3790; 642. The one at the top is worked with 647.

- Now work the bead flowers using the same thread and beads as in step 42.

44. Finally, to the right of the project and starting from the left, work the pebbles with the following threads: 640; 3790; 647. Work the bead flowers using the same thread and beads as in step 42.

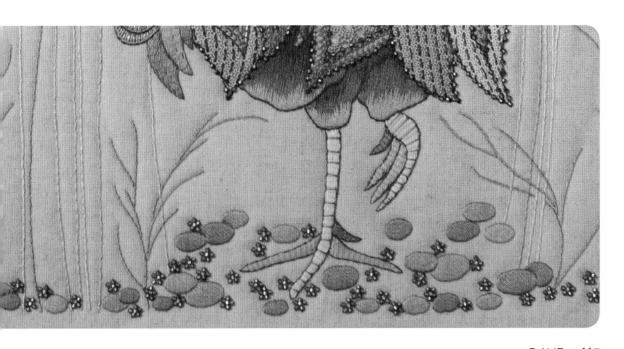

Kevin

This project is based on the traditional Chinese depiction of
a pheasant, a bird often interchanged with the phoenix as an
emblem of beauty and good fortune in Chinese culture.
The project measures 310 x 280 mm (12½ x 11").

Materials

Fabric

450 x 450 mm (18 x 18") medium-weight cotton-twill
base fabric, colour Ecru

450 x 450 mm (18 x 18") off-white cotton-voile
backing fabric x 2

450 x 450 mm (18 x 18") 100 gsm polyester or
cotton batting

Embroidery frame

2 pairs 17" Edmunds stretcher bars

Needles

Size 7 Embroidery needles
Size 10 Embroidery needles
Size 11 Sharps quilting needles
Size 26 Tapestry needles

Threads and beads

DMC STRANDED COTTON

5	Light Driftwood
6	Medium Light Driftwood
7	Driftwood
8	Dark Driftwood
13	Medium Light Nile Green
19	Medium Light Autumn Gold
30	Medium Light Blueberry
31	Blueberry
32	Dark Blueberry
33	Fuchsia
34	Dark Fuchsia
35	Very Dark Fuchsia
340	Medium Blue Violet
341	Light Blue Violet
601	Dark Cranberry
603	Cranberry
604	Light Cranberry
746	Off White
911	Medium Emerald Green
913	Medium Nile Green
954	Nile Green
955	Light Nile Green
962	Medium Dusty Rose
3021	Very Dark Brown Grey
3716	Very Light Dusty Rose
3746	Dark Blue Violet
3805	Cyclamen Pink
3806	Light Cyclamen Pink
3823	Ultra Pale Yellow
3854	Medium Autumn Gold
3855	Light Autumn Gold
3865	Winter White x 4

DMC DENTELLES #80

369	Very Light Pistachio Green
954	Nile Green

MIYUKI BEADS

2g	15° 4238	SL Paris Pink
2g	15° 4247	SL Peony Pink
2g	15° 4248	SL Dark Lilac
2g	15° 4250	SL Taupe

PRECIOSA 2MM GLASS PEARLS

1g	Cream

General instructions

- Refer to the general project instructions on
  page 19.

Stitching instruction

*Throughout this design you will be instructed to finish off sections with outlines. This will be done with stitches as described in each section, but you should not work these outlines until all the surrounding embroidery has been done.

1. Using two strands of thread throughout, fill the beak of the bird with chain stitch – interlaced variation 1. Use 3854 for the chain stitch and the small side straight stitches on either side. Use 3855 for the interlacing and, with the same thread *outline the visible edges with whipped backstitch.

2. Using two strands of 3865, outline the centre of the eye with split backstitch. With a single strand of the same thread, work satin stitch in a circle. Start each stitch on the outside of the split backstitch, finishing in a point in the centre. Attach a single bead 15° 4250 in the centre of the eyeball. Pad the semicircle that surrounds the eyeball with stem stitch using two strands of 8. With the purl edge facing outwards, work striped buttonhole stitch over the padding with a single strand of the same thread. Work the straight stitches between the buttonhole stitches with the same thread. *Outline the bottom edge and outside the purl edge with outline stitch using a single strand of 3021.

3. The crest is worked with lines of beaded backstitch. Working from the left, use a doubled-over single strand of thread and beads in the following combinations: 33/15° 4248, 33/15° 4248, 33/15° 4247, 33/15° 4247, 33/15° 4248. Using the image on the left as your guide, work additional fine lines of outline stitch in between with single strands of 32 and 913.

4. The green centre of the neck that is highlighted in the image above, is filled with what I am calling shaded trellis with cross-stitch couching variation 1 (see page 46). Use a single strand of 954 to work the trellis over the entire area. Thereafter, with a single strand each of 913, 954 and 13, work the cross stitches starting with 913 in the darker corners between the neck feathers on the right, gradually changing to 954 in the medium dark areas and then 913 for the lightest areas on the left.

5. Work the throat feathers on the left with beaded backstitch using a doubled-over strand of 7 and bead 15° 4250 for the two on the left. For the remaining three, use a doubled-over strand of 8 and bead 15° 4250. Using the colour image as your guide, work additional fine lines of outline stitch in between with single strands of 604 and 601.

6. Moving to the opposite side of the neck, work the inside feathers first. Each feather is filled with beaded wheatear stitch variation (see page 53). Use two strands of 33 for the wheatear stitch and two strands of 341 for the inward-facing straight stitches. Use a doubled-over single strand of 33 to stitch on beads 15° 4248. *Outline each feather with outline stitch using a single strand of 35.

7. The feathers to the right are filled with Van Dyke stitch variation (see page 48). Starting from the top feather and working to the bottom, use two strands of thread in the following combinations of Van Dyke stitch/straight stitches: 31/913; 30/13; 31/913; 30/13. *Outline each feather individually with outline stitch using a single strand of 32.

8. The small pink feather on the extreme right is filled with chain stitch – interlaced variation 1. Use 604 for the chain stitch and the small side straight stitches on either side. Use 603 for the interlacing and with a single strand of 601 *outline the visible edges with outline stitch.

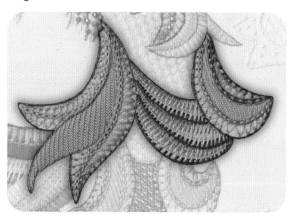

9. For the feathers at the base of the neck, start on the right with the project facing upwards as in the image above, fill the centre of the feather with needle-weaving texture no. 5-1. Use Dentelles #80 369 for colour 1, the warp stitches and #80 954 for colour 2, the weft stitches. Work chain stitch – interlaced variation 2 (see page 34) on either side of the woven centre. On the top side use two strands of 31 for the chain stitch and side straight stitches interlaced with two strands of 913. On the bottom side use two strands of 30 for the chain stitch and side straight stitches interlaced with two strands of 13. *Outline the feather with outline stitch using a single strand of 32.

10. Moving left, the three horizontally worked areas are filled with layered buttonhole stitch. Using two strands throughout, start in the upper-most set close to the neck. Work a row each with 7, 6 and 5. Moving down, repeat this for the second and third sets. To finish off, work a row on the bottom edge of each set using two strands of 8, working close to the previous row in each instance so that you create the impression of an outline.

11. Moving further left, fill this feather with interlaced chain stitch. Using two strands of 340 for the chain and side straight stitches, work the interlacing with 341. The section on the right of the feather is worked in variation 1. Start the left side following the guidelines for variation 1 (see page 34) and where it joins the feather to the left of it use basic interlacing (see page 32). *Outline the feather with outline stitch using a single strand of 3746.

12. The feather to the left of this is worked with needle-weaving texture no. 5-2 (mirror image). Use Dentelles #80 369 for colour 1, the warp stitches and #80 954 for colour 2, the weft stitches. *Outline the feather with outline stitch using a single strand of 911.

13. The final, far left feather highlighted in the image on the left is worked with interlaced chain stitch following the instructions set out in step 11 above. Using two strands, work the chain and side straight stitches with 603 doing the interlacing with 604. *Outline the feather with outline stitch using a single strand of 601.

14. Start by filling the purple centre of this area with trellis couching with triangular filling (see page 47) using single strands of thread.

- Work the trellis vertically and horizontally with two strands of 33.
- The thread woven through the couching stitches to create the triangles is 34.
- Work parallel semi-circle lines of whipped backstitch on the edge of the trellis using two strands of 35. With a doubled-over strand of the same thread, stitch single beads 15° 4248 at evenly spaced intervals between the lines.

15. Using two strands of 3855, work split backstitch around the outside perimeter of the semi-circle at the base of the triangular trellis. Working from the outside of the split backstitch, fill the semi-circle with long and short stitch shading using a single strand of the same thread. Using a single strand of 3854, work basic trellis couching over the shading and, with the same thread, *outline the outside edge with outline stitch.

16. Fill the curved feathers on either side of the triangular trellis middle following the guidelines set out in step 9 above.

17. The feathers radiating out from the bottom of this fruit are all worked with interlaced chain stitch variation 1 working from left to right, using two threads as set out below. Each feather is outlined with outline stitch using a single strand of thread

From left to right:	Chain stitch and small side stitches	Inter–lacing	Outline stitch
Feathers 1, 5	3855	19	3854
Feather 2, 4	3746	341	3756
Feather 3	3805	3806	601

18. Work the four large feathers highlighted in the image above from right to left in the loop, weaving and pistil stitch combination (see page 41) and *outline with outline stitch using the threads set out in the table below:

From right to left:	Loop stitch two strands	Weaving two strands	Pistil stitch two strands	Outline stitch single strand
Feather 1	33	34	34	35
Feather 2	954	955	913	911
Feather 3	3855	3855	19	3854
Feather 4	340	341	3746	3746

19. The small pink feather on the extreme left is filled with chain stitch – interlaced variation 1 (see page 34). Use 3805 for the chain stitch and the small straight stitches on either side. Use 3806 for the interlacing and with a single strand of 601 *outline the visible edges with outline stitch.

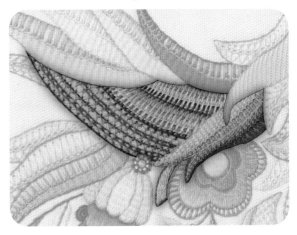

20. Moving down, the two horizontally worked sets are filled with layered buttonhole stitch as set out in step 10 above.

21. Below that are two sets of chain stitch – interlaced variation 1. Start by working a line of whipped backstitch down the solid centre line using two strands of 32. Thereafter, work chain and side straight stitches down the dotted lines of both sets. There is only one set of straight stitches between the two rows of chain stitch and these should lie over and at right angles to the whipped backstitch line in the centre. Work the interlacing with 954 using the straight stitches over the middle line for both sides. *Outline the bottom edge with whipped backstitch using two strands of 32.

22. The two feathers to the right are worked with the loop, weaving and pistil stitch combination (see page 41), using the threads in the table below:

	Loop stitch two strands	Weaving two strands	Pistil stitch two strands	Outline stitch single strand
Yellow feather	3855	3855	19	3854
Pink feather	3805	3806	601	601

23. Moving to the left and below where you have been working and starting with the top, green feather, fill this with interlaced chain stitch – variation 1 using two strands of 913 for the chain and side stitches, with 954 for the interlacing. *Outline the visible edges with outline stitch using a single strand of 911.

24. The pink feather below that is worked in the same way using two strands of 3805 for the chain and side stitches, with 603 for the interlacing. *Outline the visible edges with outline stitch using a single strand of 601.

25. Fill the feather below with the loop, weaving and pistil stitch combination (see page 41), using 30 for the loop stitch, 31 for the weaving and 913 for the pistil stitches. *Outline the feather with outline stitch using a single strand of 32.

26. Fill each of the green calyx leaves with single weaving with stranded cotton (see page 45), working the straight stitch ladder horizontally over the shortest side and weaving vertically along the length of each leaf. Use 955 for the centre leaf, 954 for the leaves on either side of the centre and 913 for the two outside leaves. *Outline each leaf with outline stitch using a single strand of 911.

27. With a doubled-over strand of 35, stitch a single 2 mm pearl over the small dot in the circle at the base of the calyx. With the same thread, work a circle of nine beads 15° 4248 around the pearl (see page 51). When you have finished couching the circle into place and using the same thread, work single small French knots adjacent to the gaps between the beads.

28. Moving to the flower, work a line of split backstitch on the semi-circular line that forms the outside of the main body of the flower. Working from outside the split backstitch fill the main body with long and short stitch shading starting with 34 at the base shading up to 33 at the tip. *Outline the upper, visible edge with outline stitch using a single strand of 35.

29. Using two strands of the relevant colour, pad each of the small circles on the outside edge of the flower with horizontal satin stitch. Thereafter, work a buttonhole half-circle over the padding coming in and down to the edge of the main body with a single strand of thread. Use 35 for the lowest circles on either side, 34 for the circles just above those and 33 for the two at the top. Stitch a single bead 15° 4248 into the base of each semi-circle.

36. Outline the bottom of this satin-stitched shape with whipped backstitch using two strands of 911. Thereafter, work the vein and *outline the entire shape in the same way.

30. Starting with the blue and green motif highlighted in the image above, pad the circle in the centre with horizontal satin stitch using two strands of 913. With a single strand of the same thread, work horizontal satin stitch over the padding.

31. Moving out from the centre, pad the first scalloped area with stem stitch using two strands of 32. With a single strand of the same thread, work close buttonhole stitch over the padding.

32. Pad the scalloped area on the outside of that with stem stitch using two strands of 31. Work vertical and fanned long and short stitch shading over the padding starting with 31 at the base shading up to 30 on the outside edge.

33. Finally, work striped buttonhole stitch around the final scalloped edge. Use 32 for the buttonhole stitch and 954 for the straight stitches.

34. Moving to the green motif below that and following the instructions in step 4 (see page 121), use a single strand of 954 to work the trellis over the entire area. Thereafter, with a single strand each of 954, 955 and 13, work the cross stitches starting with 954 closest to the curve at the top, slowly changing to 955 in the middle and then 13 for the light area closest to the scalloped edge.

35. Pad the outside, scalloped edge on the left side with stem stitch that runs along the length of the shape with two strands of 913. Work satin stitch over and in the opposite direction to the padding with a single strand of the same thread, fanning the stitches around the shape.

37. Each section of the branch is worked in the same way. Using two strands of 8, start a section of branch by doing a row of stem stitch up the outer line on one side. Now stitch back down, still doing stem stitch, immediately adjacent to the line you have just stitched. From the third row and every now and then, instead of doing a stem stitch, do a bullion knot, and then continue stem stitching as before. Continue doing these adjacent lines of stem stitch, substituting with bullions from time to time. Once you have completed the main threadwork, and to enhance the gnarled look of the branch, use two strands of 3021 to work a French knot against some of the bullion knots, pushing the bullion into a curve as you complete the French knot.

> **Tip:** It is these bullion knots that give the branch its gnarled appearance. But don't be tempted to do too many bullion knots and ensure that they are evenly spread over each section of the branch.

38. *Outline the visible edges on the top and bottom of the branch with outline stitch using a single strand of 3021.

39. Fill the legs and feet with single weaving shading using a single strand of 19. Referring to the colour image, *outline the legs and feet with whipped backstitch using two strands of 3854.

using a single strand of 8, continuing the stitch down to work the shorter, and the main stems.

43. Fill the large leaf with long and short stitch shading using single strands of thread. Starting close to the vein and working each side separately, use 913 shading through 954 to 13 on the edge. With a single strand of 911 and using the image above as your guide, *work intermittent outlines with outline stitch. Work the vein, continuing along the branch all the way to the bud, with whipped backstitch using two strands of 8. Work beaded backstitch on the small side branch with a doubled-over strand of 7 and bead 15° 4250.

40. All of the small leaves, the bud petals and the bud calyxes are worked according to the instructions for satin stitch leaf (see page 44). Using two strands throughout and working from the bud on the top right in the image above, use 3806 for the bud, 955 for the smaller leaf and 954 for the bigger one. With a single strand of 601, define the left side the petal and the vein with outline stitch. With a single strand of 8, work outline stitch down the vein of each calyx leaf. The bud to the left of that uses 3805 for the petal, 955 for the calyx leaf on the right and 913 for the one on the left. The bud on the extreme left in the image above uses 3805 for the petal, 954 for the calyx leaf on the right and 955 for the one on the left. Work the petal outline and all veins in the same way as you did for the first bud described.

41. At the base of each bud, bead couch a 2 mm cream pearl and a bead 15° 4250 using a doubled-over strand of thread 8. For the buds on the right, continue stitching whipped backstitch down the short stems using the same thread.

42. Moving to the branch of small leaves and working from the top, use two strands of thread for the leaves as follows: 954 on the right and 913 in the left, 955 on the left and 954 on the right, 955 at the bottom. Work the veins with outline stitch

44. Moving to the two branches on the left of where you have been working, work the two lazy daisy strawberries (see page 40) using two strands each of 962 for the darker pink, followed by 3716 for the lighter pink rows. Thereafter use 746 for the lighter yellow and 3823 for the darker yellow at the top. The French knots are worked in 3854. The satin stitch leaves at the top of the fruit are worked, from the left, using two strands of 913, 955, 954 and 13. Using a single strand of 911, and referring to the image before to guide you, *work outline stitch along one side of each leaf, finishing off with a single short stitch going down from the point on the other side of the leaf.

45. Moving to the fuchsia on the left:

- Pad each of the two blue areas that make up the corolla with vertical stem stitch, using two strands of 30. With a single strand of the same thread, work horizontal satin stitch over the padding. Thereafter, work basic trellis couching over the satin stitch using a single strand of 32 and, with the same thread, work outline stitch on the outer edges of each blue segment. The pink sepals below and facing into the corolla are worked with raised herringbone stitch using two strands of thread. Use 3806 for the middle and 3805 for the side sepals. *Outline each one with outline stitch using a single strand of 601.
- Pad the ovary below the sepals with horizontal satin stitch using two strands of 913. With a single strand of the same thread, work vertical satin stitch over the satin stitch padding. *Outline the top edge with outline stitch using a single strand of 911.
- Pad the tube of the flower below the ovary with horizontal satin stitch using two strands of 3806. Work long and short stitch shading over the padding, starting with 3805 at the base, shading up to 3806 at the tips. With a single strand of 601, work basic trellis couching over the shading and, with the same thread, *outline the tube with outline stitch.
- Work the calyx leaves at the base of the tube with raised herringbone stitch using two strands of 13. *Outline each leaf with outline stitch using a single strand of 911.
- Work the three stamens at the tip of the flower with outline stitch using a single strand of 32. Place a single bead 15° 4238 at the tip of each stamen.

46. Moving to the purple flower:

- Pad each petal of the flower separately with horizontal satin stitch, using two strands of 34.
- Using single strands of thread, work long and short stitch shading over the padding of each petal, facing in towards the centre. Start at the base with 34 shading to 33 at the tip.
- Except for the centre, work basic trellis couching over the whole flower, using a single strand of 35 and with the same thread, define the sides and outer edge of each petal with outline stitch.
- With a doubled-over strand of 35, stitch a single 2 mm pearl in the centre of the flower. With the same thread do a circle of 10 beads 15° 4248 (see page 51) around the pearl. When you have finished couching the circle into place, use the same thread to work small single French knots adjacent to the gaps between the beads.
- Using two strands of 913, work the small leaves with raised herringbone stitch (see page 39). Outline each leaf with outline stitch using a single strand of 911.

47. Fill the large leaf below the purple flower with long and short stitch shading using single strands of thread. Starting close to the vein and working each side separately, use 913 shading through 954 to 955 on the edge. With a single strand of 911 and using the image above as your guide, *work intermittent outlines with outline stitch.

48. Work the vein, continuing along the branch all the way up to the top, with whipped backstitch using two strands of 8. Work all of the other branches, and sections of the branches in this section in the same way.

49. The small leaves that are attached to the branches are worked as satin-stitch leaves, as you did in 44 before. The leaf attached to the branch above the top left strawberry is worked with 955. Those attached to the branch on the right of this are worked, from the top, with 913, 954, 955, 913, 954 and 955. The veins are worked, as you did before, but in this instance with outline stitch using a single strand of 8.

50. Moving down the project and starting with the fuchsia highlighted in the above image:

- Work vertical stem stitch padding in each of the two blue areas that make up the corolla, using two strands of 341. With a single strand of the same thread, work horizontal satin stitch over the padding. Thereafter, work basic trellis couching over the satin stitch using a single strand of 3746 and, with the same thread, work outline stitch on the outer edges of each blue segment. The pink sepals below and facing into the corolla are worked with raised herringbone stitch using two strands of thread. Use 604 for the middle and 603 for the side sepals. *Outline each one with outline stitch using a single strand of 3805.
- Pad the ovary below the sepals with horizontal satin stitch using two strands of 913. With a single strand of the same thread, work vertical satin stitch over the satin-stitch padding. *Outline the top edge with outline stitch using a single strand of 911.
- Pad the tube of the flower below the ovary with horizontal satin stitch using two strands of 604. Work long and short stitch shading over the padding starting with 603 at the base, shading up to 604 at the tips. With a single strand of

3805, work basic trellis couching over the shading and, with the same thread, *outline the tube with outline stitch.
- Work the calyx leaves at the base of the tube with raised herringbone stitch using two strands of 13. *Outline each leaf with outline stitch using a single strand of 911.
- Work the three stamens at the tip of the flower with outline stitch using a single strand of 3746. Place a single bead 15° 4238 at the tip of each stamen.

51. Moving to the yellow flower:
- Pad each petal of the flower separately with horizontal satin stitch, using two strands of 3855.
- Using single strands of thread, work long and short stitch shading over the padding of each petal, facing in towards the centre. Start at the base with 3855 shading to 19 at the tip.
- Except for the centre, work basic trellis couching over the whole flower, using a single strand of 3854 and with the same thread, define the sides and outer edge of each petal with outline stitch.
- With a doubled over strand of 35, stitch a single 2 mm pearl in the centre of the flower. With the same thread and following the instructions for bead circles in the bead embroidery gallery, do a circle of 10 beads 15° 4248 around pearl. When you have finished couching the circle into place and using the same thread, work small single French knots adjacent to the gaps between the beads.
- Using two strands of 913, work the small leaves with raised herringbone stitch (see page 39). Outline each leaf with outline stitch using a single strand of 911.

52. Work the small segment of the branch leading up from the flower and also that little bit above the fuchsia with whipped backstitch using two strands of 8.

53. Work the strawberry as described in step 44 on page 126.

54. Work the fuchsia as described in step 45 on page 27.

55. Work the shaded leaf as described in step 47 on page 127.

56. Work the vein, continuing along the short section of branch, with whipped backstitch using two strands of 8. Work all of the other branches, and sections of the branches in this section in the same way. Work the curved side branches with beaded backstitch using a doubled over strand of 7 and bead 15° 4250.

To turn this project into the page of a book as I have done, if you did not add the batting and additional voile backing from the beginning, you should now remove the project from the frame.

- Place a layer of voile, then a layer of batting, then the project so far back over the frame and secure it all together, making sure that you stretch all of the layers as you go. There should be no folds visible on the back of the work. Everything smooth and well secured.
- The entire background is stitched with 3865. The stitching is worked with two strands, **unless otherwise stated**.

57. Starting with the motif at the top left of this project:

- Fill the large centre of the motif with trellis with cross stitch couching variation 1 (see page 46) using a single strand of thread.
- Continuing with two strands of thread, work a bullion knot on each of the radiating lines within the centre.
- Work reverse chain stitch on each of the vertical lines within the middle, pointed area. Work evenly spaced French knots between the parallel lines. Outline the two sides of the pointed area with heavy chain stitch.
- Fill the inside of the calyx with trellis couching with cross-stitch filling (see page 46) using a single strand of thread. Continuing with two strands of thread, outline each section of the calyx with heavy chain stitch.
- Work each tendril that comes out of the left of the calyx with backstitch/French knot combination (see page 27).
- Moving to the border around the main part of the motif, work heavy chain stitch on the inner line and reverse chain stitch on the outside line. Work intermittent, evenly spaced French knots between the two lines.
- Work reverse chain stitch on the outlines of each of the three small leaves at the top of the motif with a buttonhole circle (see page 29) on the circle below those leaves.

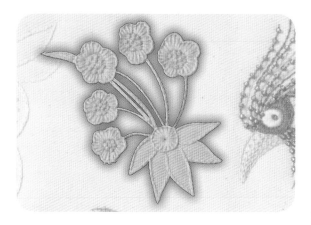

58. Moving to the right of the motif you have just done:

- The lower line of the main branch leading down to the circle and leaves at the bottom is worked with heavy chain stitch. The upper line is worked with reverse chain stitch. The five flower stems are worked with whipped backstitch.
- Each of the small flowers is a buttonhole flower (see page 29). Fill the centre of each flower with seven to ten French knots.
- Work reverse chain-stitch on the outlines of each of the five small leaves at the bottom of the motif with a buttonhole circle on the circle at the base of these leaves.

59. Starting with the branch that comes out of the bottom of the motif that you worked in step 57:

- Work the tendril with a backstitch/French knot combination.

- The inside line on the right is worked with heavy chain stitch while the outside, left line is worked with reverse chain stitch.

60. Moving to the top section of the large leaf, the bottom of which is described later:

- Fill the centre with seeding using a single strand.
- Continuing with two strands, work the vein that runs up the middle of the seeding with heavy chain stitch.
- Work the lines adjacent to the top edge of the seeding with heavy chain stitch. The outside lines of this edge are worked with reverse chain stitch.
- Moving to the area below the seeding, work the two elongated crescent shapes with blanket stitch, the purl edges in both facing towards the bottom of the project. To define the bottom edge of both, work reverse chain stitch adjacent to the bottom of the blanket stitching. In the case of the crescent adjacent to the seeding, continue working the reverse chain stitch to the tip of the leaf. Where the other is concerned, work the reverse chain stitch until you meet up with the purl edge of the first crescent shape. Work evenly spaced French knots in the space left between the two crescents.

61. Moving to the bottom half of the large leaf:

- Fill the centre with basic trellis couching using a single strand of thread.
- Continuing with two strands, work the veins that run up the middle of the seeding with heavy chain stitch.
- Work the lines adjacent to both sides of the edges of the seeding with heavy chain stitch. The outside lines on both sides are worked with reverse chain stitch.
- Work the tendrils on either side with a backstitch/French knot combination.

62. Moving to the motif at the bottom left of the project:

- Fill the larger, top section of the centre of the motif with trellis couching with cross stitch filling using a single strand.
- Fill the smaller, bottom section with trellis with cross stitch couching variation 1, also using a single strand of thread.
- Continuing with two strands, work loop stitch along the area between the parallel scalloped lines. Define both the top and bottom edge of the loop stitch with whipped backstitch.
- Moving to the double edge on the outside of the main central area, work heavy chain stitch on the inner outside lines adjacent to the trellis couching with cross stitch filling. Work reverse chain stitch on the outer lines and evenly spaced French knots in the space between the two lines.

- Work reverse chain stitch on each of the vertical lines within the calyx. Work evenly spaced French knots between the parallel lines. Work a buttonhole circle at the base of the calyx. Outline the top part of the calyx with heavy chain stitch.
- Moving to the top of the motif, fill each of the small petals with seeding. Outline each petal with heavy chain stitch and then work a buttonhole circle where they intersect.
- Work reverse chain stitch around each of the leaf shapes that radiate from the sides of this motif.
- Work a backstitch/French knot combination on all the tendrils that come off the main branch at the bottom of the motif.
- Work heavy chain stitch along the upper line and reverse chain stitch along the lower line of the branch.

63. Moving to the motif on the top right of the project:

- Working over all three of the petals at the same time, fill the centres with trellis couching with triangular filling (see page 47) using a single strand of thread.
- Continuing with two strands of thread, outline each petal with heavy chain stitch in as continuous a line as possible.

- Work reverse chain stitch on the outside, serrated edges of the petals and, using the previous image as your guide, work evenly spaced French knots in the space that remains.
- Work a backstitch/French knot combination on all of the tendrils.
- Moving to the branch leading up to the motif, work heavy chain stitch on the left line and reverse chain stitch on the right-hand line.

64. Moving down, still on the right of the project, complete the branch as described in the final bullet point in 63 above.

65. Moving to the small flowers:

- The five flower stems are worked with whipped backstitch. Each of the small flowers is a buttonhole flower (see page 29). Fill the centre of each flower with seven to ten French knots.

66. Moving to the top section of the large leaf, the bottom of which is described later:

- Fill the centre with seeding using a single strand.
- Continuing with two strands, work the vein that runs up the middle of the seeding with heavy chain stitch.
- Work the lines adjacent to the right-hand edge

of the seeding with heavy chain stitch. The outside lines of this edge are worked with reverse chain stitch.

- Moving to the area on the left of the seeding, work the elongated crescent shape with blanket stitch, the purl edge facing towards the outside of the leaf. To define the bottom edge, work reverse chain stitch adjacent to the bottom, inside edge of the blanket stitching. Continue working the reverse chain stitch to the tip of the leaf.

67. Work the bottom half of the leaf as described in step 61 on page 131.

68. Moving to the motif at the bottom right of the project:

- Fill the larger centre of the motif with trellis couching with cross stitch filling (see page 46) using a single strand.
- Continuing with two strands and moving to the double edge on the outside of the main central area, work heavy chain stitch on both the outside lines adjacent to the trellis couching with cross stitch filling. Work evenly spaced French knots in the space between the two lines.
- Moving to the circular shapes between the two double-lined edges and starting with the double oval shape, work a buttonhole circle on the outer, larger circle taking the bottom of the stitches in on the line of the inner circle. Work a second buttonhole circle on the inner, smaller oval shape making sure that the purl edge of that circle lays over the raw, bottom edge of the outside circle. Work a buttonhole circle on the remaining circles above the oval shape.
- Fill the middle of the semi-oval shapes on either side of the area you have just worked with seeding using a single strand of thread. Continuing with two strands, work loop stitch along the area between the parallel lines that form the edge. Define both the top and bottom edge of the loop stitch with whipped backstitch.
- Moving to the large calyx leaves at the bottom of this motif, fill the centre of each leaf with meandering running stitch using a single strand of thread.
- Continuing with two strands, work closed feather stitch around the area between the parallel lines of the border around the calyx leaves.
- The branch leading up to this motif is worked with heavy chain stitch on the lower inside line and reverse chain stitch on the upper, outside line.
- Moving to the top of the motif, outline each leaf with reverse chain stitch. The vein of each leaf, continuing down the stem to the buttonhole circles, is worked with whipped backstitch.
- Work a backstitch/French knot combination on

the lines of the tendril that comes off the side of the motif.

69. Moving to the large leaf motif on the left of where you have been working:

- Work the small flowers as described in 65 on the previous page.
- Work a backstitch/French knot combination on the lines of the curly tendril.
- Work this half of the leaf as described in 61 on page 131.

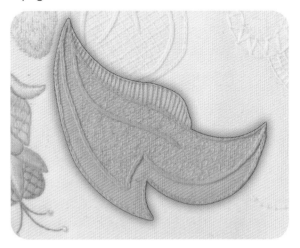

70. Work this half of the leaf as described in step 66 on the previous page.

Dick

The mallard is a duck found throughout the world either because it is indigenous or because it has been introduced. It is a duck ripe for embroidery because of its unique and beautiful colouring. This project measures approximately 290 x 290 mm (11½ x 11½") depending on whether or not you choose to add the background ripples in order to quilt the design.

Material

Fabric

450 x 450 mm (18 x 18") medium-weight linen-cotton blend base fabric, colour Natural

450 x 450 mm (18 x 18") off-white cotton-voile backing fabric x 2

450 x 450 mm (18 x 18") 100 gsm polyester or cotton batting

Embroidery frame

2 pairs 17" Edmunds stretcher bars

Needles

Size 7 Embroidery needles
Size 10 Embroidery needles
Size 11 Bead embroidery needles
Size 26 Tapestry needles

THREADS AND BEADS

DMC STRANDED COTTON

597	Turquoise
598	Light Turquoise
818	Baby Pink
911	Medium Emerald Green
913	Medium Nile Green
954	Nile Green
955	Light Nile Green
3033	Very Light Mocha Brown
3371	Black Brown
3781	Dark Mocha Brown
3782	Light Mocha Brown
3790	Ultra Dark Beige Grey (x2)
3808	Ultra Very Dark Turquoise
3809	Dark Turquoise
3810	Very Dark Turquoise
3866	Ultra Very Light Mocha Brown
4030	Monet's Garden
4150	Desert Sand
4501	Wildfowers

FINCA PERLE #16

1062	Light Golden Brown
1068	Medium Golden Brown
1137	Pale Yellow
3000	Ecru
3556	Light Turquoise
3560	Peacock Blue
3574	Dark Turquoise
3664	Very Dark Turquoise
3670	Ultra Very Dark Turquoise
4000	Dark Ecru
4379	Light Nile Green
5224	Light Khaki Green
5229	Medium Khaki Green
8083	Dark Coffee Brown
8310	Light Drab Green Brown
8327	Dark Drab Green Brown

MIYUKI BEADS

2g	15° 556	Rose Silver Lined Alabaster
2g	15° 5F	Matte Silver Lined Dark Topaz
2g	15° 2425	Silver Lined Teal

PRECIOSA VIVA 12 FLAT-BACK CRYSTALS

1 piece 20ss Smoke Topaz AB

General instruction

Refer to the general project instructions on page 19. If you are intending to quilt this design you will note, in the line drawings at the back of the book, that the ripples in the background have been provided separately. It is important that you trace these on with a washout pen, usually a Frixion pen is best, as you will be doing running stitches with a single strand of thread and you want to be able to remove the lines afterwards.

Stitching instruction

*Throughout this design you will be instructed to finish off sections with outlines. This will be done with stitches as described in each section, but you should not work these outlines until all surrounding embroidery has been done.

1. Referring to the guidelines for two-tone vermicelli couching (see page 49) fill the head of the duck using the image above to guide you.

- The middle, green area uses two strands of 954 couched with a single strand of the same thread, for the first layer.
- The second layer, worked between the first layer swirls, uses a single strand of 911 couched with a single strand of the same thread.
- The turquoise areas on either side of the head use two strands of 3810 couched with a single strand of the same thread, for the first layer.
- The second layer, worked between the first layer swirls, uses a single strand of 3808 couched with a single strand of the same thread.
- *Outline the outer visible edges, including the throat area at the bottom of the face with outline stitch using a single strand of 3808.

2. Fill the beak with needle-weaving texture no 5 - 2 mirror image (see page 68) as follows (if you

are left handed, follow the guidelines for needle-weaving texture no 5 – 1 as on page 68 so that the diagonal lines develop in the desired direction):

- Starting at the base of the beak, adjacent to the face, leaving a space for the nostril, work warp stitches using Finca perle #16 1068 until you have gone just past the start of the nostril. Continue working a few shorter warp stitches above the nostril until you get to approximately where it ends.
- Work the remaining warp stitches with Finca perle #16 1137.
- Starting at the top of the beak work the weft stitches, following the pattern, with 1068 until you have filled the beak below the hump at the top. Continue with shorter weft stitches on the right-hand side area of the nostril.
- Changing to 1137 and picking up the pattern on the left-hand side of the nostril, continue creating the twill pattern to fill the beak until you reach the darker area at the bottom.
- Complete the needle weaving using 1068.
- Using two strands of 3371, pad the nostril with horizontal satin stitch. With a single strand of the same thread, work vertical satin stitch over the padding; make sure that you cover the raw edges of the needle weaving.
- Using a single strand of 3371, work about five to six satin stitches into the small hook at the tip of the beak.
- Using two strands of 3781, outline the entire beak, not including the little hook at the front, with whipped backstitch.
- *Work a second outline around the beak with outline stitch using a single strand of 3371.

3. Moving to the eye, fill the background with single-weaving filler using a single strand of 3033. Do not work over the small circle in the eye.

- Outline the eye with whipped backstitch using two strands of 3781. *Work a second outline around the eye, outside the whipped backstitch, using a single strand of 3371 to do outline stitch.
- Following the guidelines for a caged flat-back

crystal (see page 53), stitch a 20ss smoked topaz AB crystal over the small circle using a single strand of 3371.

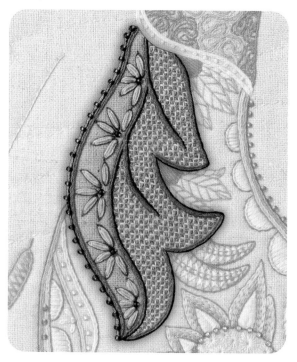

4. Moving to the neck, start with the large leaf-shaped motif on the left.

- Working in the left side of the motif, work a double bullion lazy daisy stitch (see page 29) on each of the lines that radiate out from their central points depicting half a flower. Use two strands of 4150 to work the bullion knot and the first lazy daisy stitch. Use a single strand of 3781 for the second, outer lazy daisy stitch.
- With a doubled-over strand of 3782, stitch a bead 15° 5F into the centre of each half flower.
- Fill the area to the right of the half flowers with trellis couching with cross-stitch couching variation 1 (see page 46). Using a single strand of 4150 work over the entire area, including the lines of the veins.
- Using two strands of 3790, *outline each section of this motif, including the three lines that make up the vein down the middle, with heavy chain stitch.
- Using the image above to guide you, work

outline stitch on the outside of the heavy chain stitch using a single strand of 3371. With a doubled-over strand of 3782, stitch beads 15° 5F at evenly spaced intervals down the outline on the left, going into the neck of the bird.

- With the same thread, work outline stitch on the inside edge of the three parts of the vein.

5. There are two three-petal motifs that peep out on the right of the large leaf-shaped motif. They are worked in the same way.

- Fill each of the petals separately with long and short stitch using a single strand of 4150.
- With a single strand of 3790, work a line of fly stitch over each petal. With the same thread, work outline stitch on the visible edges to define each petal.
- Fill the semi-circular shapes at the base of the petals with striped blanket stitch, making sure that the purl edge at the top of the shape lies over the raw edges at the base of the petals. Working with single strands, use 3781 for the blanket stitch and 3790 for the straight stitches in between.

6. Work both of the two feather-shaped motifs that peep out on the right at the bottom of the large leaf shape in the same way.

- Fill each shape with interlaced chain-stitch – variation 1 (see page 34) using two strands of 3790 for the chain stitch and the little side straight-stitches. Work the interlacing with two strands of 4150.
- Using a single strand of 3781, outline the visible edges of each shape with outline stitch.

7. Moving now to the right side, start with the semi-circular shapes that run down the length of the neck. With the purl edge on the rounded side,

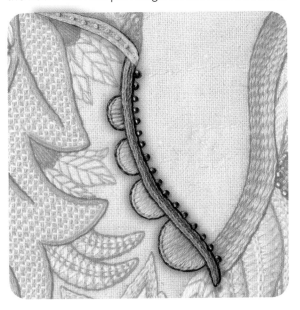

work striped blanket stitch in each semi-circle. Working with two strands, use 4501 for the blanket stitch and 818 for the straight stitches. With a single strand of 3808, work outline stitch adjacent to the purl edge of each semi-circle.

8. Moving to the petals that are below the semi-circles, fill each one separately with long and short stitch using a single strand of 4150. With a single strand of 3790, work a line of fly stitch over each petal. With the same thread, work outline stitch on the visible edges to define each petal.

9. Now work the double outline that forms the outside edge of the neck.

- Using two strands of 913, work heavy chain on

the inside line of the double line that goes down the length of the neck. With a single strand of 3808, work outline stitch on the outside edge adjacent to the heavy chain stitch.

- Using two strands of 3790, work heavy chain stitch on the outside line of the double line that goes down the length of the neck. *With a single strand of 3371, work outline stitch on the outside edge adjacent to the heavy chain stitch line. With a doubled-over strand of 3782, stitch beads 15° 5F at evenly spaced intervals down the outer edge of the outline stitch.
- When you have completed the double lines down the side of the neck, moving up, work the double lines at the base of the vermicelli couching on the head with heavy chain stitch using two strands of 3866. Make sure that the lines cover any raw edges at the bottom of the vermicelli couching and at the top of the leaf motif described in step 4. With the same thread, work single-wrap French knots at evenly spaced intervals between the double lines.

10. Moving down the body, continue stitching on the left side.

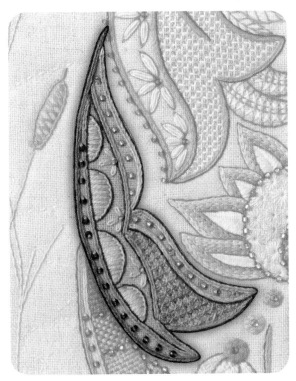

- With the purl edge on the rounded side, work striped blanket stitch in each semi-circle. Working with two strands, use 4501 for the blanket stitch and 818 for the straight stitches. With a single strand of 3808, work outline stitch adjacent to the purl edge of each semi-circle.
- On each of the small dots above the semi-circle and with a doubled-over strand of 818, stitch a bead 15° 556 surrounded with three lazy daisy petals.

11. The shaped area in the lower middle area of the motif is filled with trellis – cross stitch couching variation 1 (see page 46), using a single strand of 4030.

- Each line that makes up the curved double outline on the right of this shape is worked in heavy chain stitch using two strands of 4501. Continue the heavy chain stitch on the outside edge of the top section only.
- On the bottom edge of the trellised area, up the side of it and on the inside line of the top section, work heavy chain stitch with two strands of 913. Using the same thread and continuing to work heavy chain stitch, complete the line leading down to the point as well as the line that runs adjacent to the striped blanket stitch circles.
- Stitch beads 15° 556 on the dots between the double lines on the right using a doubled-over strand of 818. With a single strand of 3808, work outline stitch adjacent to the outside of the heavy chain stitch lines on the right side of the motif. Work the outline stitch facing to the inside in the area filled by the striped blanket stitch semi-circles.

12. Starting at the lower tip of the motif and using two strands of 3781, work heavy chain stitch up the left side eventually joining up with the outline worked in step 4 (see page 138). Work outline stitch on the outside of the heavy chain stitch using a single strand of 3371. With a doubled-over strand of 3782, stitch beads 15° 5F on the dots depicted between the brown and the green heavy chain stitch double lines.

13. Moving further down the body of the bird, fill each of the semi-circular shapes with basic double-weaving (see page 64). For the #16 thread colours listed below, the warp runs from the top to the bottom whilst the weft goes from the left to the right of each semi-circle.

- Starting with the smallest wedge-shaped semi-circle at the top, work the warp stitches with 3574 and the weft stitches with 3670.
- The second semi-circle uses 3670 for the warp and 3560 for the weft stitches.
- The third semi-circle uses 3560 for the warp and 3664 for the weft stitches.
- The fourth semi-circle uses 3664 for the warp and 3556 for the weft stitches.
- The fifth semi-circle at the bottom uses 3556 for the warp and 4379 for the weft stitches.
- Using a doubled-over strand of 3808 and bead 15° 2425, work beaded backstitch around the outside of each semi-circle.

14. Moving along, fill the leaf shape with single-weaving shading using a single strand of 4030. Outline the outside edge with outline stitch using a single strand of 3808.

15. Work a line of heavy chain stitch on each of the double lines below the leaf shape, using two strands of 4501. In the space between that and the outer body double outline, with a doubled-over strand of 818, stitch three beads 15° 556 evenly spaced and surrounded, to the extent that you can fit them in, with lazy-daisy petals. Using a single strand of 3808, work outline stitch adjacent to the outside edges of the heavy chain stitch.

16. Work the double body outline with heavy chain stitch as you did in step 12 using 913 on the inside, 3781 on the outside and beads 15° 5F evenly spaced between the double lines. Outline the outside edge of the brown line with outline stitch using a single strand of 3371 and the inside edge of the green line using a single strand of 3808.

17. Moving to this floral motif in the middle of the body, start with the woven semi-circle in the middle of the flower.

- Following the guidelines for checks and stripes no. 8 (see page 66), use 3670 for colour 1 and 3664 for colour 2. *Outline the outside edge with beaded backstitch using a doubled-over strand of 3808 and bead 15° 2425.
- Fill the crescent shape that surrounds the middle section with eye-stitch variation (see page 37) using a single strand of 4501. *Outline the outside edge with beaded backstitch using a doubled-over strand of 3808 and bead 15° 2425.

- Fill the centre of each of the leaf shapes that radiate from the top of the flower with raised herringbone stitch using two strands of 3866. Using two strands of 3810, work chain stitch around and adjacent to each centre. Using two strands of 598, work chain stitch on the outside line of each leaf shape. Fill in any remaining space between the lines of chain stitch with lines or half lines of chain stitch using two strands of 597. Using a single strand of 3808, work outline stitch in the ditch between the centres and the outside chain stitched edges of each leaf shape. Using the same thread, outline each leaf with outline stitch.
- The three leaves of the calyx are filled with long and short stitch shading. Starting at the base of each leaf, using single strands of thread, use 3866 shading through 954 to 955 at the tip. Using a single strand of 913, work basic trellis couching (see page 45) over the shading. Using a single strand of 3808, outline each leaf with outline stitch.

18. Each of the three petals of the little flower is filled with long and short stitch shading overlaid with basic trellis couching, using a single strand of 4501. With a single strand of 3808, outline each petal with outline stitch.

19. All of the circles in the image above are woven spider's web circles (see page 50) with a bead 15° 2425 in the centre. The circle at the base of the three-petal flower is worked with 3809. The one above that is worked with 598 and the third one in that line is done with 597. Moving to the other side of the floral motif, use 597 for the circle at the top, 598 for the one below the calyx leaf and 3809 for the circle at the bottom.

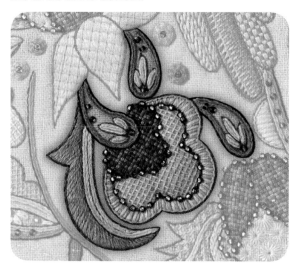

20. Start with the flower shape, working from the base and starting with the needle weaving.

- Following the guidelines for checks and stripes no. 8 (see page 66), use 3670 for colour 1 and 3664 for colour 2. *Outline the outside edge with beaded backstitch using a doubled-over strand of 3808 and bead 15° 2425.
- Moving out, fill the central section of the flower with single-weaving shading (see page 44) using a single strand of 4501. *Outline the outside edge with beaded backstitch using a doubled-over strand of 3808 and bead 15° 2425.
- Pad the outside border with continuous lines of stem stitch using two strands of 3866. Work striped blanket stitch over the padding using two strands of thread, 913 for the blanket stitch and 3866 for the straight stitches. *Outline the outer edge with outline stitch using a single strand of 3808.

21. The main section of the leaf shape that curls up on the left side of the flower is filled with long and short stitch shading. Using single strands of cotton, start adjacent to the vein with 3810 shading to 597 at the outer edges. Work the double

lines of the vein with heavy chain stitch using two strands of 4501. *Outline the entire leaf with outline stitch using a single strand of 3808. With the same thread, work outline stitch in the ditch between the shading and the vein.

22. The three paisley shapes are worked in the same way.

- Work a bullion lazy-daisy stitch – double (see page 29) on each of the lines that radiate out from the central point at the base of the shape. Use two strands of 4150 to work the bullion knot and the first lazy-daisy stitch. Use a single strand of 3781 for the second, outer lazy-daisy stitch.
- With a doubled-over strand of 3782, stitch a bead 15° 5F into the centre of the three-petal flower. At the same time, stitch single beads onto the two dots at the tip of the shape.
- Work a line of heavy chain stitch on the line around each shape using two strands of 3790. Work a line of outline stitch on the outside of the heavy chain stitch using a single strand of 3371.

23. Moving to the lower part of the body, start with the floral motif.

- Working the calyx leaves following the guide-lines for checks and stripes no. 8 (see page 66), use 3670 for colour 1 and 3664 for colour 2. *Outline the outside edge with beaded back-stitch using a doubled-over strand of 3808 and bead 15° 2425.
- Moving out, fill the centre of the flower with eye-stitch variation using a single strand of

4501. *Outline the outside edge with beaded backstitch using a doubled-over strand of 3808 and bead 15° 2425.

- To work the outside border and using two strands of 913, work a line of chain stitch adjacent to and all the way around the centre of the flower. Work a line of chain stitch that abuts the existing line using two strands of 954. Using two strands of 955, work a line of chain stitch on the line that forms the outside of the border. Fill in any remaining space with lines, or half lines, of chain stitch using 955. *Outline the outer edge with outline stitch using a single strand of 3808.

24. Now work the leaf that curls out from this flower.

- Fill the main body of the leaf with trellis – cross-stitch couching variation 1 (see page 46), using a single strand of 4030.
- Using two strands of 4501, work a line of heavy chain stitch up the vein. Work a line of outline stitch adjacent to the upper edge of the vein.
- With the same thread, outline the leaf with outline stitch.

25. Moving to the tail, fill the centre of the bottom part of the tail with semi-circles of double weaving.

- Starting with smallest wedge-shaped circle at the base of the tail, work the warp stitches with 3574 and the weft stitches with 3670.
- The second semi-circle uses 3670 for the warp and 3560 for the weft stitches.
- The third semi-circle uses 3560 for the warp and 3664 for the weft stitches.

- The fourth semi-circle uses 3664 for the warp and 3556 for the weft stitches.
- Using a doubled-over strand of 3808 and bead 15° 2425, work beaded backstitch around the outside of each semi-circle.

26. Work the double outline at the bottom with heavy chain stitch as you have done previously using 913 on the inside, 3790 on the outside, beads 15° 5F evenly spaced between the double lines. Outline the outside edge of the brown line with outline stitch using a single strand of 3371 and the inside edge of the green line using a single strand of 3808.

27. Fill the leaf shape below the floral motif described in step 23 with single-weaving shading using single strands of cotton. Use 3790 for the warp stitches and 3781 for the weft stitches. Outline the visible edge of the leaf with outline stitch using a single strand of 3781.

28. Work heavy chain stitch on the line that starts within the body and extends towards the tip of the tail using two strands of 3790. Outline the lower edge with outline stitch using a single strand of 3371.

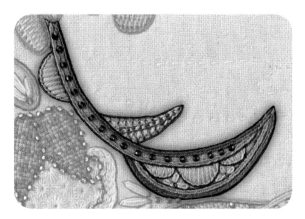

29. Fill the centre of the top of the tail following the instructions in the first part of step 10 (see page 140). Outline the bottom edge with heavy chain stitch using two strands of thread, 913 for the inside line and 3790 for the outside line. Using single strands outline the outside edge of the brown line with 3371, and the inside of the green line with 3808 with outline stitch.

30. Work a double bullion lazy-daisy stitch on each of the lines that radiate in from the tail. Use two strands of 4150 to work the bullion knot and the first lazy-daisy stitch. Use a single strand of 3781 for the second, outer lazy daisy stitch. With a doubled-over strand of 3782, stitch a bead 15° 5F into the centre of the three-petal flower. At the same time, stitch single beads onto the two dots below that.

31. Move up the tail slightly to the feather shaped motif that peeps out from the body. Fill the shape with interlaced chain-stitch – variation 1 (see page 34) using two strands of 3790 for the chain stitch and the little side straight-stitches. Work the interlacing with two strands of 4150. Using a single strand of 3781, outline the visible edge of each shape with outline stitch.

32. Moving up slightly to the semi-circle inside the body, work striped blanket-stitch with two strands of thread, using 4501 for the blanket stitch and 818 for the straight stitch. Outline the outer edge with outline stitch using a single strand of 3808.

33. Work the double outline from the base of the wing to the tip of the tail with heavy chain stitch, as you have done previously, using 913 on the inside, 3790 on the outside, beads 15° 5F evenly spaced between the double lines. Outline the outside edge of the brown line with outline stitch using a single strand of 3371 and the inside edge of the green line using a single strand of 3808.

34. Both webbed feet are worked in the same way. Each yellow section is filled with needle-weaving texture no. 5 with a variation (see page 69) in the direction of the diagonal lines that develop in the pattern. This will depend on whether you follow the guidelines for the no. 1 or the no. 2 (mirror image) variation, as follows:

- Work the warp stitches of the front section with Finca perle #16 1137. Work the weft stitch using perle #16 1068 following the guidelines for texture 5 – 2 (mirror image). If you are left-handed, follow the guidelines for texture 5 – 1.

- Work the warp stitches of the middle section with perle #16 1062 and the weft stitches using perle #1068 following the guidelines for texture 5 – 1. If you are left-handed, follow the guidelines for texture 5 – 2 (mirror image).

- Work both the warp and weft stitches of the back section with perle #16 1068 following the guidelines for texture 5 – 1. If you are left-handed, follow the guidelines for texture 5 – 2 (mirror image).

- Work whipped backstitch on the lines that separate each section of the feet using two strands of 3790. With a single strand of 3371, work outline stitch around each section of the feet, including the front ends. This stitch should be worked adjacent to the upper side of the whipped backstitch, with the exception of the line that runs along the bottom of the bottom section. This should be worked adjacent to the lower side.

35. Fill the short legs of the duck with basic single-weaving – bird's leg variation (see page 65). Turn the work sideways so that you work the warp stitches in the pattern over the shortest side with the weft stitches going the length of the leg. Use #16 8327 for colour 1 and #16 4000 for colour 2. *Outline the three visible edges of the leg with outline stitch using a single strand of 3371.

36. Starting with the long section on the left of the highlighted area in the image on page 145 (top left), follow the guidelines for whipped chain stitch variation (see page 35).

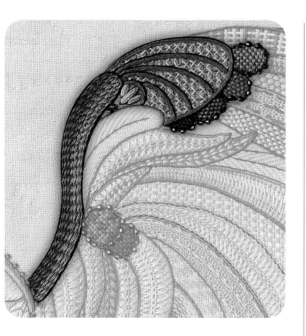

38. Fill the shell shaped section to the left of the area that you have just worked with trellis – cross-stitch couching variation 1 (see page 46). Using a single strand of 4150 work over the entire area, including the lines within the shape.

- Using two strands of 3790, work heavy chain stitch on the lines within the shape and *outline the visible edge of this motif, including the small curved bit at the bottom, with heavy chain stitch. With a single strand of 3371, work outline stitch adjacent to the upper side of the lines within the shape, on the outside of the motif outline and on the inside of the small curved bit at the bottom.

39. Between the section described in step 36 and step 40 below are three lines and two dots that should be worked as described in step 30 (see page 144).

- Working along the length of the area, from base to tip work four rows using two strands of 3790 for the chain stitch and a single strand of 3781 for the whipping.
- Work one row of chain stitch using two strands of 3782, whipping with a single strand of 3781 on the left, where the colours change.
- Work a further three or four rows using two strands of 3782, whipping with a single strand of 3790.
- *Outline the visible edges with outline stitch using a single strand of 3371.

37. Fill the semi-circles on the right of the shell shape with double weaving.

- Starting with the smallest semi-circle at the base, work the warp stitches with 3574 and the weft stitches with 3670.
- Moving up, the second semi-circle uses 3670 for the warp and 3560 for the weft stitches.
- The third semi-circle uses 3560 for the warp and 3664 for the weft stitches.
- The top, fourth semi-circle uses 3664 for the warp and 3556 for the weft stitches.
- *Using a doubled-over strand of 3808 and bead 15° 2425, work beaded backstitch around the outside of each semi-circle.

40. Starting with the top left-wing feather highlighted in the image above, follow the instructions for weaving a twill feather following on from texture no. 5 (see page 71).

- Using perle #16 for the warp stitches, work them over the shortest side from the tip of the feather down to the base. As you go, fan them ever so slightly on each stitch so that they go with the direction of the feather.

- Work the weft stitches with perle #16 3000.
- Using a single strand of 3781, work outline stitch up the vein in the centre, stopping short of the tip as shown in the image before.
- With the same thread, *outline the visible edges of the feather with outline stitch.

41. Working from the top, above the two turquoise circles, fill the remaining feathers highlighted in the image above as follows:

- The top feather is worked with interlaced chain stitch variation 1 (see page 34), using two strands of 3782 for the chain stitch and side straight-stitches and two strands of 4150 for the interlacing. Using a single strand of 3790, *outline the visible edges of the feather with whipped backstitch. With a single strand of 3781, work outline stitches adjacent to the outside of the whipped backstitch.
- The feather next to and extending beyond the one you have just filled is worked with wheatear stitch variation (see page 49). Use two strands of 3790 for the wheatear stitch and two strands of 4150 for the centre back stitches and the diagonal side stitches.
- Fill the feather immediately above the two turquoise circles with interlaced chain stitch variation 1, using two strands of 3790 for the chain stitch and side straight-stitches, and two strands of 4150 for the interlacing. Using a single strand of 3790, *outline the visible edges of the feather with whipped backstitch. With a single strand of 3781, work outline stitches adjacent to the outside of the whipped backstitch.

42. Moving to the feathers below the two turquoise circles, starting from the top, fill the three feathers with interlaced chain stitch variation 1 using the following threads:

- The top feather uses 3782 for the chain and side stitches with 3033 for the interlacing.
- The middle feather uses 4150 for the chain and side stitches with 3033 for the interlacing.
- The bottom feather uses 3790 for the chain and side stitches with 3033 for the interlacing.

- Using a single strand of 3790, *outline the visible edges of each feather with whipped backstitch. With a single strand of 3781, work outline stitches adjacent to the outside of the whipped backstitch.

43. Now fill the two turquoise circles with needle weaving.

- For the inside circle follow the guidelines for checks and stripes no. 8 (see page 66); use perle #16 3670 for colour 1 and perle #16 3664 for colour 2.
- For the outside part-circle work basic double-weaving using perle #16 3670 for the warp and 3574 for the weft stitches.
- *Outline the outside edge of both circles with beaded backstitch using a doubled-over strand of 3808 and bead 15° 2425.

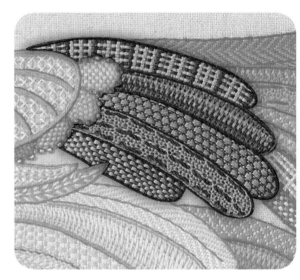

44. To work the top wing feather in the section highlighted above, refer to the guidelines for basic double-weaving - duck wing step 44 (see page 64), using the colours listed. Using two strands of 3781 *outline the top and the rounded tip of this feather with whipped backstitch.

45. The next feather down is worked with layered buttonhole stitch (see page 31). Work each row starting at the base of the feather moving towards the tip.

- Start at the bottom with two rows using two strands of 3790.

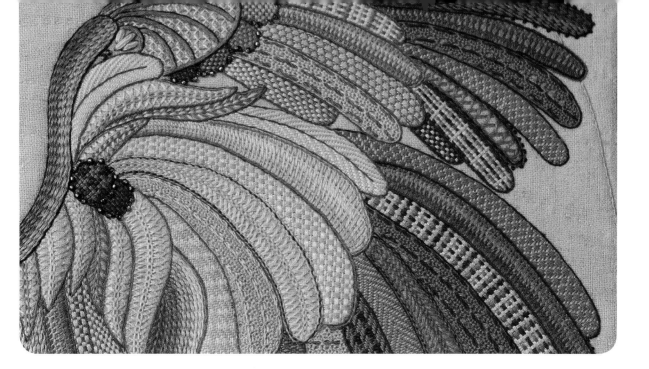

- Work the next two rows with two strands of 3782.
- The final row is worked close to the previous row, using two strands of 3790. When you get to the tip of the feather, continue working around the curve, doing two stitches where you would have done one so that it will curve around without being too tight and taking the bottom end of the stitch into the spaces between the downward strokes of the existing buttonhole stitches in each row, to the bottom.
- With a single strand of 3781, work outline stitch between the ridge, or purl, of the last and the second last row of buttonhole stitch.

46. Fill the next feather down with needle-weaving texture no. 2 (see page 67) using #16 8327 for the warp and #16 4000 for the weft stitches. Using two strands of 3781 *outline the top and the rounded tip of this feather with whipped backstitch.

47. Fill the penultimate feather in this section with needle lace following the guidelines for Dick wing filler (see page 61). Use #16 8310 for the detached buttonhole stitches and a doubled-over single strand of #16 8327 to make the twisted cord (see page 50). Whip the anchoring backstitch around the feather with #16 8310. Using two strands of 3781 *outline the top and the rounded tip of this feather with whipped backstitch.

48. Fill the bottom feather highlighted in the image on page 146 with needle-weaving checks and stripes no. 13 (see page 66). Use #16 8327 for colour 1, #16 8310 for colour 2 and #16 4379 for colour 3. Using two strands of 3781 *outline the bottom and the rounded tip of this feather with whipped backstitch.

49. Moving down the inside wing area, fill the top feather highlighted in the above image following the instructions for weaving a twill feather as in step 40 (see page 145).

50. Fill the next feather following the instructions for the layered buttonhole feather as in step 45 (see page 146). Starting from the bottom and using two strands of thread, work two rows using 3782 and two rows using 3033. Work the final row close to the row below that with 3790 going around the curve as you did before. With a single strand of 3781, work outline stitch between the ridge, or purl, of the last and the second last rows of buttonhole stitch.

51. Fill the next feather with needle-weaving texture no. 9 (see page 71). Referring to the image before to guide you use #16 3000 for the downward warp stitches and #16 4000 for the horizontal weft stitches. Using two strands of 3790 *outline the top and the rounded tip of this feather with whipped backstitch. Thereafter, using a single strand of 3781, work outline stitch on the inside of the whipped backstitch.

52. Following the guidelines for chain stitch – interlaced, double (see page 33), starting at the base and using two strands of thread, fill the next feather using 3782 for the rows of chain stitch, 3033 for the interlacing and a single strand of 3781 for the backstitch 'outline'.

53. Moving down, fill the next feather with Dick wing-filler as you did in step 47. Use #16 8310 for the detached buttonhole stitches and a doubled-over single strand of #16 4000 to make the twisted cord. Whip the anchoring backstitch around the feather with #16 8310. Using two strands of 3781 *outline the bottom and the rounded tip of this feather with whipped backstitch.

54. The next feather down appears on the right of the section highlighted in the image above. Following the guidelines for needle-weaving checks and stripes no. 1 (see page 66), use #16 8310 for colour 1 and #16 3000 for colour 2, working the warp stitches over the shortest side. Using two strands of 3790 *outline the left side and the rounded tip of this feather with whipped backstitch. Thereafter, using a single strand of 3781, work outline stitch on the inside of the whipped backstitch.

55. Moving left, the next feather is worked with whipped chain stitch variation (see page 35) in much the same way as you did the spine described in step 36 (see page 145).

- Starting on the left of the space working from base to tip, do a third of the space – three to four rows – using two strands of 3790, whipping the sides of the rows together with a single strand of 3781. Work the next third of the space with two strands of 3782 for the chain stitch, whipping with a single strand of 3790. Where the two colours meet at the beginning, whip with the darker 3781. The final third is worked with 3033, whipped with 3782. Once again, where the two colours meet whip with the darker colour.
- Before working the outline, fill the small space on the left with wheatear-stitch variation using two strands of 3781 for the wheatear stitch and

3782 for the additional side stitches and the backstitch down the middle.

- Finally, using two strands of 3781, work a whipped backstitch outline around the curved tip of what is essentially both of the feathers.

56. Moving left, the next two feathers are worked with interlaced chain stitch variation 1 (see page 34) using two strands of the following threads:

- The feather on the right uses 3033 for the chain and little side-stitch along with 4150 for the interlacing.
- The feather on the left uses 3782 for the chain and little side-stitch along with 3033 for the interlacing.
- * Outline the visible edges of the feathers with whipped backstitch using two strands of 3790. With a single strand of 3781, work outline stitch on the outside of each line of whipped backstitch.
- Fill the small feather to the left with wheatear-stitch variation using two strands of 3790 for the wheatear stitch and 3782 for the additional side stitches and the backstitch down the middle. * Outline the small visible edges on the left with whipped backstitch using two strands of 3790. With a single strand of 3781, work outline stitch on the outside of the line of whipped backstitch.

57. Starting on the right, fill that feather with needle-weaving checks and stripes no. 13 (see page 66). Use #16 8327 for colour 1, #16 8310 for colour 2 and #16 4379 for colour 3. Using a single strand of 3781 *outline the entire feather with outline stitch.

58. Fill the next feather to the left with basic double-weaving using perle #16 8327 for the warp stitches and #16 8310 for the weft. Using a single strand of 3781 *outline the visible edges of the feather with outline stitch.

59. Fill the next feather following the instructions for the layered buttonhole feather set out in step 45 (see page 146). Starting from the bottom, or right-hand side of the feather, and using two strands of thread, work two rows using 3790 and two rows using 3782. Work the final row close to the row before that with 3790, going around the curve as you did before. With a single strand of 3781, work outline stitch between the ridge, or purl, of the last and the second last row of buttonhole stitch.

60. Moving left, the next feather is worked with whipped chain stitch variation in much the same way as you did the spine described in step 36 (see page 145). Starting on the right of the space and working from base to tip, do half of the space – two rows – using two strands of 3782, whipping the sides of the rows together with a single strand of 3790. Work the remaining half of the space with two strands of 3033 for the chain stitch and continue the whipping with a single strand of 3790. Using a single strand of 3781 *outline the visible edges of the feather with outline stitch.

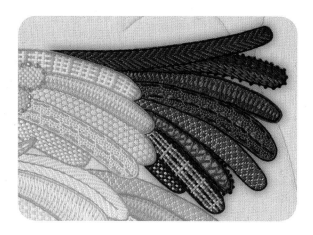

61. Starting with the top wing feather highlighted in the image above, follow the instructions for weaving a twill feather following on from texture no. 5 (see page 71). Using perle #16 8083 for the warp stitches, work them over the shortest side from the tip of the feather down to the base. As you go, fan them ever so slightly on each stitch so that they go with the direction of the feather. Work the weft stitches with perle #16 8327. Using a single strand of 3371, *outline the feather with outline stitch.

62. Moving down, fill the next feather with whipped chain stitch variation in much the same way as you did the spine described in step 36 (see page 144). Starting at the top of the space, working from base to tip, do half of the space – three rows – using two strands of 3781, whipping the sides of the rows together with a single strand of 3371. Work the remaining half of the space with two strands of 3790 for the chain stitch and continue the whipping with a single strand of 3371. Using a single strand of 3371 *outline the visible edges of the feather with outline stitch. With the same thread and referring to the colour image above, work evenly-spaced single-wrap French knots adjacent to the outer edge of the outline stitch.

63. Fill the next feather following the instructions for the layered buttonhole feather as in step 45 (see page 146). Starting from the bottom, or right-hand side of the feather, and using two strands of thread, work two rows using 3781 and one row using 3790. Work the final row close to the row

before that with 3781, going around the curve as you did before. With a single strand of 3371, work outline stitch between the ridge, or purl, of the last and the second last row of buttonhole stitch.

64. Moving down, fill the next feather with Dick wing-filler as in step 47 (see page 147). Use #16 8327 for the detached buttonhole stitches and a doubled-over single strand of #16 8083 to make the twisted cord. Whip the anchoring backstitch around the feather with #16 8327. *Using a single strand of 3371, work outline stitch adjacent to the whipped backstitch.

65. Moving down, fill the next feather with needle-weaving texture no. 2 (see page 67) using #16 4000 for the warp and #16 8327 for the weft stitches. *Using a single strand of 3371 work outline stitch one the visible edges of this feather.

66. The feather below this is filled with the simpler version of chain stitch – interlaced, double (see page 33). Use two strands of 3790 for both the chain stitch and the interlacing. Use a single strand of 3371 to work the backstitch 'outline'. With the same thread and using the image above to guide you, work evenly-spaced single-wrap French knots adjacent to the outer edge of the chain stitch.

67. To work the next wing feather in the section highlighted above, refer to the guidelines for basic double-weaving – duck wing steps 67 and 71 (see page 65), using the colours listed. Using #16 8083 *outline the bottom and the rounded tip of this feather with whipped backstitch.

68. Fill the bottom feather highlighted in the above image with needle-weaving checks and stripes no. 13 (see page 66). Use #16 8083 for colour 1, #16 8327 for colour 2 and #16 4379 for colour 3. Using #16 8083 *outline the bottom and the rounded tip of this feather with whipped backstitch.

69. Fill the top feather highlighted in this section following the instructions in step 65.

70. Fill the next feather following the instructions for the layered buttonhole feather as in step 45 (see page 146). Starting from the bottom and using two strands of thread, work two rows using 3781 and two rows using 3790. Work the final row close to the row before that with 3781, going around the curve as you did before. With a single strand of 3371, work outline stitch between the ridge, or purl, of the last and the second last row of buttonhole stitch. With the same thread and referring to the colour image above, work evenly-spaced single-wrap French knots adjacent to the chain stitch only where the edge is exposed at the tip of the feather.

71. To work the next wing feather in the section highlighted above, follow the guidelines for basic double-weaving – duck wing steps 67 and 71 (see page 65), using the colours listed. Using #16 8083 *outline the top and the rounded tip of this feather with whipped backstitch. With a single strand of 3371, work evenly-spaced single-wrap French knots adjacent to the whipped backstitch only where the edge is exposed at the tip of the feather.

72. Fill the next feather with needle lace as in step 64 (see page 150).

73. For the feather below the needle lacing, use the guidelines for chain stitch – interlaced, double (see page 33). Start your work at the base and using two strands of thread, fill this feather using 3781 for the rows of chain stitch, 3790 for the interlacing and a single strand of 3371 for the backstitch 'outline'. With the same thread and referring to the colour image above, work evenly-spaced single-wrap French knots adjacent to the chain stitch only where the edge is exposed at the tip of the feather.

74. To work the next wing feather highlighted in the image on the left, follow the instructions for weaving a twill feather following on from texture no. 5 (see page 69). Using perle #16 4000 for the warp stitches, work them over the shortest side from the tip of the feather down to the base. Work the weft stitches with perle #16 8327. Using a single strand of 3371, *outline the small exposed tip of the feather with outline stitch.

75. The last little feather highlighted in the image on the left is worked following the guidelines for needle-weaving checks and stripes no. 1 (see page 66). Use #16 8083 for colour 1 and #16 8327 for colour 2, working the warp stitches over the shortest side. Using a single strand of 3371, *outline the entire feather with outline stitch.

76. Working from the right of the highlighted bits in the image above, fill the first feather with Dick wing-filler (see page 61) working from tip to base.

Use #16 3556 for the detached buttonhole stitches and a doubled-over single strand of #16 3664 to make the twisted cord. Whip the anchoring back-stitch around the feather with #16 3556. Using a single strand of 3808 *outline the visible edge with outline stitch.

77. The next small feather to the left is worked with needle-weaving texture no. 2 (see page 67). Work the warp stitches over the short side using #16 3560. Use #16 3570 for the weft stitches and with a single strand of 3808 *outline the visible edge with outline stitch.

78. Fill the next feather with needle-weaving checks and stripes no. 13 (see page 66). Use #16 3670 for colour 1, #16 3664 for colour 2 and #16 3556 for colour 3. Using a single strand of 3808 *outline the visible edge with outline stitch.

79. To work the next feather to the left, follow the instructions for weaving a twill feather following on from texture no. 5 (see page 71). Using perle #16 3670 for the warp stitches, work them over the shortest side from the tip of the feather down to the base. Work the weft stitches with perle #16 4379. Using a single strand of 3808 *outline the visible edge with outline stitch.

80. Fill the next feather following the instructions for the layered buttonhole feather in step 45 (see page 146). Starting from the base of the feather and using two strands of thread, work three rows using 3808, followed by three rows worked with 3810 and then three rows with 597. Work the final row close to the row before that with 3808. With the same thread, *work a whipped backstitch outline around the visible edge of the feather.

81. Fill the last small feather with needle-weaving texture no. 9 (see page 71). Working over the short side, use #16 3556 for the warp stitches and 3670 for the weft stitches. Using a single strand of 3808 *outline the visible edge with outline stitch.

If you are intending to turn this project into the page of a book as I have done, and you did not add the batting and additional voile backing from the beginning, you should now remove the project from the frame.

Place a layer of voile, then a layer of batting, then the project so far back over the frame and secure it all together, making sure that you stretch all of the layers as you go. There should be no folds visible on the back of the work. Everything should be smooth and well secured.

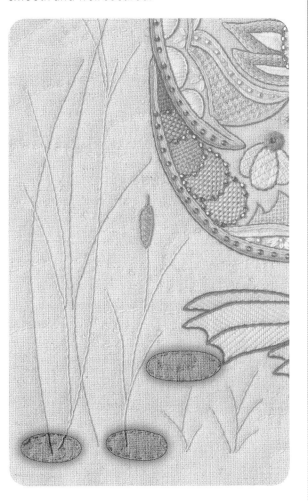

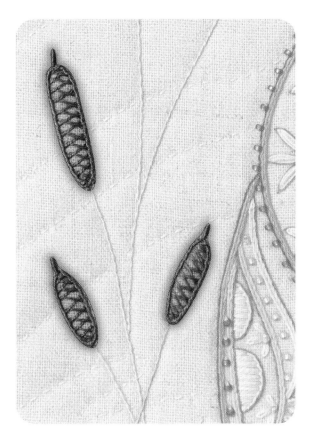

82. Although they are barely visible in the colour images of this project, you will have traced the ripples onto the background if you are intending to quilt the project. Work all of the lines with running stitch using a single strand of 4150. The small whirlpools at the base of the design should be worked with running stitch using a single strand of 4030.

83. Fill each of the shapes that represent the bulrush with interlaced herringbone-stitch using two strands of 3790. Whip the backstitch that holds the interlacing and finish off with a small, four-wrap bullion to represent the stamen at the tip.

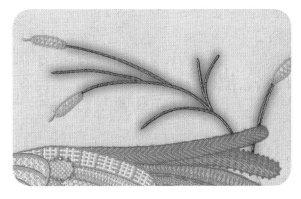

84. All of the bulrush stems and leaves are worked in whipped backstitch. Use #16 5229 for the stems and #16 5224 for the leaves that come off the stems.

Nigel

The name of this bird is derived from the Spanish word flamengo that means 'flame-coloured'. There are six flamingo species which, between them, are native to most of the continents, barring Australia and Antarctica. Their distinctive colouring comes from the carotenoids in their diet of crustaceans and algae. This project measures approximately 305 x 275 mm (12½ x 11").

Materials

Fabric

450 x 450 mm (18 x 18") medium-weight linen-cotton blend base fabric, colour natural

450 x 450 mm (18 x 18") off-white cotton-voile backing fabric x 2

450 x 450 mm (18 x 18") 100 gsm polyester or cotton batting

Embroidery frame

2 pairs 17" Edmunds stretcher bars

Needles

Size 7 Embroidery needles
Size 10 Embroidery needles
Size 11 Bead Embroidery needles
Size 26 or 28 Tapestry needles

Threads and beads

DMC STRANDED COTTON

ECRU	Ecru
310	Black
413	Dark Pewter Grey
414	Dark Steel Grey
644	Medium Beige Grey x 4
967	Very Light Apricot
3708	Light Melon
3799	Very Dark Pewter Grey
3824	Light Apricot
3831	Dark Raspberry
3832	Medium Raspberry
4110	Sunrise

FINCA PERLE #16

1301	Very Light Apricot
1895	Dark Melon
1889	Medium Melon

MIYUKI BEADS

4g	#1 2442 Crystal Ivory Gold Luster
2g	15° 458 Metallic Brown Iris
4g	15° 2442 Crystal Ivory Gold Luster
4g	15° 4239 Silver Lined Hibiscus
2g	8° 401F Matte Black

General instruction

- Refer to the general project instructions on page 19.

Stitching instructions

*Throughout this design you will be instructed to finish off sections with outlines. This will be done with stitches as described in each section, but you should not work these outlines until all surrounding embroidery has been done.

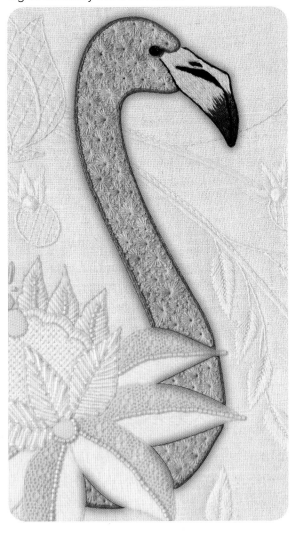

1. Using a single strand of 4110, fill the neck and face with eye-stitch variation.

- Move from one to the next using the same strand of thread. Don't make them too round or too square. Make them different sizes and don't concentrate on keeping all of the stitches in the eye the same length. Irregular is good.

- Fill in spaces between the eye stitches with single-wrap French knots.
- Repeat this technique with the same thread in the areas between the floral elements in the body of the bird.
- *Outline the outer edges of the face and neck with whipped backstitch using two strands of 3832. Continue this outline around the area that makes up the eye.

2. Following the guidelines for attaching a bead with a bead (see page 51) and using a doubled-over strand of 310, make the eye with a large bead 8° 401F held down with a smaller bead 15° 458.

3. The beak is filled with long and short stitch shading using single strands of thread.

- Start at the bottom – or tip – of the beak with 3799. Leave a very tiny, hardly visible gap when you reach the line that divides the two sides of the beak. Using the image above as your guide, shade to 413.
- Change to 3824, shading into the grey for the width of the left side of the beak and for about half of the width of the right side.
- Complete the rest of the right side using 967 shading into the grey, and do another row or two on that side with the same colour.
- Still using 967, shade the left side of the beak to approximately level with where the middle line of the beak ends.
- Leaving space for the nostril on the right side, fill the remaining space on both sides using a single strand of Ecru.
- Using a single strand of 310 and starting at the bottom, work outline stitch up the centre line of the beak. When you get to the top, work rows down and up, filling in the wider part. While you're up there, work a couple of rows in the nostril and then, going back to the centre line, work outline stitch from the top all the way down to the bottom.

4. Still using a single strand of 310 and using the image above as your guide, *outline the beak with outline stitch.

5. Moving to the floral elements of the body, start with the larger flower closest to the neck.

- The darker side of each leaf is filled with needle-lace stitch 1 variation filler (see page 58). Use perle #16 1895. With the same thread, whip the backstitch on the outside edge of that half of the leaf.

- Fill the other side of each leaf with long and short stitch shading using single strands of thread. Working from the vein out to the edge, start with 3824 shading through 967 to 3708. *Using a single strand of 3832, outline the outside edge of the shading with outline stitch.

- Using a doubled-over strand of 3831 and beads 15° 4239, bead couch a line of beads along the vein of the leaf.

6. Moving to the top of the flower, work from the right. Fill the three petals on the right and the first left of the centre with beaded fly-stitch with variation (see page 52). Use a doubled-over single strand of 3832 and bead 15° 4239 for the fly stitch and two strands of 3824 for the straight stitches on each side. *Outline each petal with outline stitch using a single strand of 3831.

7. Fill the middle area of the next two petals on the left with beaded fly stitch with variation using the same threads and bead. Outline the fly-stitched area and the outside lines of each petal with reverse chain stitch using two strands of 3832. Using a doubled-over strand of 3831, stitch single beads 15° 4239 at evenly-spaced intervals between the lines of reverse chain stitch. Using a single strand of the same thread, *work outline stitch adjacent to the outside edge of the outer line of reverse chain stitch.

8. Still moving around the left side of the flower, the next petal is worked in two halves.

- Fill the top half with striped up and down buttonhole stitch (see page 31). Use two strands of 3832 for the up and down buttonhole stitch and two strands of 3824 for the straight stitches.

- Fill the bottom half of the petal with long and short stitch shading using single strands of

thread. Working from the vein out to the edge, start with 3824 shading through 3824 to 3708. *Using a single strand of 3832, outline the outside edge of the shading with outline stitch.

- Using a doubled-over strand of 3831 and beads 15° 4239, bead couch a line of beads along the vein of the leaf.

9. Fill the main section of the remaining petal with beaded fly-stitch with variation using the same threads and bead that you used in step 6. Outline the bottom of the fly-stitched area and the bottom outside line with reverse chain stitch using two strands of 3832. Using a doubled-over strand of 3831, stitch single beads 15° 4239 at evenly-spaced intervals between the lines of reverse chain stitch. Using a single strand of the same thread, *work outline stitch adjacent to the outside edge of the outer line of reverse chain stitch, continuing the outline on the outer edge of the top side of the fly stitch.

10. Fill the main, middle area of the flower with woven trellis couching (see page 47), using two strands of thread throughout; use Ecru for shade 1, 3708 for shade 2 and 3824 for shades 3 and 4.

11. Using two strands of 967, pad the side areas with lines of stem stitch worked along the length of each side. With the purl edge facing to the outside, work striped blanket stitch over the padding using 3832 for the blanket stitch and 967 for the straight stitches in between. Using two strands of

3832, work lines of whipped backstitch in the ditch between the striped blanket stitch sides and the woven trellis centre.

12. Fill the circles at the top with basic single-weaving (see page 65). Use perle #16 1889 for the lower, larger circle and 1895 for the circle above that one. *Using a single strand of 3831, work fine outline stitch around each circle. With a doubled-over strand of the same thread, stitch single beads 15° 4239 on the three dots above the smaller circle. Using two strands of 3832, work a bullion knot on the two lines above the single beads. With two strands of 3831, work a detached chain stitch around each bullion knot.

13. Move down to the three leaves at the bottom of the area highlighted in the image above.

- Start by filling the circle in the middle with basic single weaving using perle #16 1889.
- Referring to the image on the left, bead couch lines of beads onto each of the dotted lines in the leaves. Use a doubled-over strand of 3708. Starting each line on the outside edge, pick up a single bead 15° 2442, a single bugle bead #1 2442 and between one and three beads 15° 2442.
- Using two strands of 3824, work one or two straight stitches between bead-couched lines.
- Using perle #16 1895, work the vein and the outline of each leaf with whipped backstitch.
- With a doubled-over single strand of 3831, bead couch a semi-circle of beads 15° 4239 on the bottom edge of the woven circle at the base of the leaves.

14. Moving left along Nigel's body, work the base of the next flower.

- Fill the bottom section of each of the side calyx leaves with needle-lace stitch 1 variation filler (see page 58) using perle #16 1301.
- Moving to the top sections of the side leaves and the middle leaf, bead couch lines of beads onto each of the dotted lines. Use a doubled-over strand of Ecru. Starting each line on the outside edge, pick up a single bead 15° 2442, a single bugle bead #1 2442 and between one and three beads 15° 2442.
- Using two strands of 967, work stem stitch between the bead-couched lines.
- Fill the circles at the bottom of the calyx with basic single-weaving using perle #16 1889 for the larger and #16 1895 for the small circle. *Outline the bottom circle with outline stitch using a single strand of 3831. With a doubled-over strand of the same thread, bead couch a semi-circle of beads 15° 4239 on the bottom edge of the larger circle.
- When you have completed the stitching described in the next section and using perle #16 1895, work the vein and the outline of each calyx leaf with whipped backstitch. The single beads on the outer edge at the tip of the right side calyx leaf will be described later.

15. Move to the top of the flower.

- Fill the area in the middle with long and short stitch using a single strand of Ecru.
- Work trellis couching with cross-stitch filling (see page 46) over the long and short stitch using a single strand of 3824 for the lines of the trellis and 3708 for the straight stitches that make up the cross at each intersection.

16. Moving to the wide border around the shading, bead couch lines of beads onto each of the dotted lines.

- Use a doubled-over strand of Ecru. Starting each line on the inside edge, pick up a single bead 15° 2442, a single bugle bead #1 2442 and one or two beads 15° 2442. Where the lines meet the pointed segment of the calyx leaf, pick up just two of the size 15° beads.
- With two strands of 3824, work bullion knots between the lines of bead couching.
- Using #16 1895, work whipped backstitch in the ditch between the shaded area and the bead couched/bullion knot edge. Outline the outer edge with whipped backstitch using the same thread.
- Using a doubled-over strand of 3831, stitch single beads 15° 4239 on the dots that start on

the part of the wide border that is the outside of the body, continuing to the tip of the right side calyx leaf mentioned in step 14.

17. Fill the two leaves that come out of the bottom side of this flower with beaded fly-stitch variation following the guidelines in step 6 (see page 158).

18. Move to the flower that embellishes the back end of Nigel's body.

- Fill the areas on each side of the middle calyx leaf with horizontal long and short stitch shading using a single strand of Ecru.
- Work trellis with cross-stitch couching variation 2 (see page 46) over the shading. Use a single strand of 3824 for the trellis and 3708 for the cross stitch.
- *Outline the outside edge of each area with whipped backstitch using two strands of 3832.

19. Fill the half-ring with striped blanket stitch (see page 31). With the purl edge facing outwards use two strands, with 3832 for the blanket stitch and 3824 for the straight stitches. Outline the inner edge with whipped backstitch using two strands of 3832.

20. With a doubled-over strand of 3831, stitch single beads 15° 4239 on the dots on the outside of the ring.

21. Fill the middle leaf with needle-lace stitch 1 variation filler (see page 58) using perle #16 1895. Start in the narrow area at the base of the petal working rows of detached buttonhole stitch until you get to a point towards the tip that is wide enough to work the pattern of holes. You will get one 'flower' into the space along with a single hole after that before you reach the tip. Outline the visible edges with whipped backstitch using the same thread.

22. Fill the two leaves on either side of the needle-lace leaf with beaded fly-stitch variation following the guidelines in step 6 (see page 158).

23. Now work the calyx.

- Fill the circle at the base of the calyx with basic single-weaving using perle #16 1889. Outline the bottom of the circle with bead couching using a doubled-over single strand of 3831 and beads 15° 4239.
- *When you have completed the leaves, outline the rest of the circle with whipped backstitch using #16 1895.

24. Using the image before as your guide, work vertical bead-couching on the lines in the calyx leaves using a doubled-over strand of 3708.

- Start each leaf by working the middle line with beads 15° 2442 and #1 2442. Start and try to end with round beads, varying them in between.
- With two strands of 3824, work stem stitch between the lines of beads.
- *Outline each leaf with whipped backstitch using perle #16 1895.

25. Fill the middle of the leaf with needle-lace stitch 1 variation filler using perle #16 1895. *Outline the visible edges with whipped backstitch using the same thread.

26. Work the outer part of the leaf with bead couching using a doubled-over strand of 3708 and beads 15° 2442 and #1 2442. Start and end with round beads varying them in between. With two strands of 3824, work stem stitch between the lines of beads.

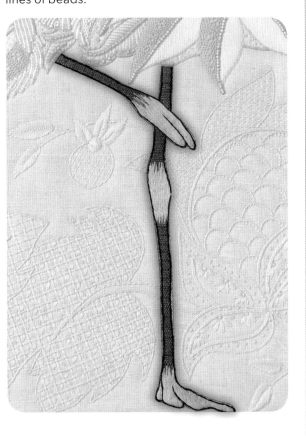

27. Start with the knee area in the full leg on the right.

- Doing long and short stitching shading with single threads, work from the middle of the knee. Do two rows using 967. Thereafter, shade out to a single row on each side using 3824.
- You will need to do a second row of shading on each side but before you do that, move to the foot as instructed in the next step.

28. Using the image above as your guide, work both feet with long and short stitch shading using single threads.

- Work a little of each toe using 3824, shading into 967 and then back to 3824 as you get into the transition from the leg to the foot.

29. You will need to do a second row of shading with 3824 but before you do that start working the leg as instructed below.

- Following the guidelines for single-weaving shading (see page 44) and using single strands of thread, work the warp stitches horizontally across the short side of each section of the leg. Work sets of five stitches with 414 and one stitch with 413, going all the way down to just above the first row of shading worked with 3824. For the lower leg on the right, start just below the first row of shading at the bottom of the knee, continuing down to just above the first row of shading in the foot.
- Now finish the second row of shading with 3824 on either side of the knee and the top of each foot.
- To complete each section of the leg, work the weft stitches of the single weaving using 414. Where the weft stitches meet up with, or start from the areas of shading, treat them as you would if you were doing normal shading. In other words, start or end the stitches randomly, longer or shorter, taking them into the second row of 3824 shading.

30. With a single strand of 310, outline each section of the leg and each toe with outline stitch using the image above to guide you.

If you are intending to turn this project into the page of a book as I have done, and you did not add the batting and additional voile backing from the beginning, you should now remove the project from the frame.

Place a layer of voile, then a layer of batting, then the project so far back over the frame and secure it all together, making sure that you stretch all of the layers as you go. There should be no folds visible on the back of the work. Everything should be smooth and well secured.

All the background elements are worked with stranded cotton 644.

chain stitch on the bottom lines and ordinary chain stitch on the top lines. Where the branch narrows as it goes into the fruit, transition from working ordinary chain stitch to a few split stitches to reduce the width of the tip of the branch.

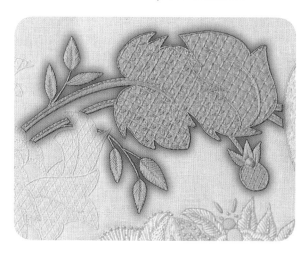

31. Start with the berries.

- Using a single strand of thread, work basic trellis couching over the round area that forms the actual fruit.
- Fill the small circle at the top of the fruit with Rhodes stitch (see page 43) using two strands of thread.
- Following the guidelines for a satin-stitch leaf (see page 44), fill each of the small leaves at the top. Start at the tip of each leaf with a straight stitch, working down on either side until you meet up with either the circle in the middle or the edge of the berry on either side.
- Using two strands of thread and starting from the edge of the small Rhodes stitch circle on one side, work a whipped backstitch outline around the main part of the berry, meeting up with the other side of the small circle.

32. Fill the leaves that come off the main stem with fly stitch. Start at the tip of the leaf with a straight stitch continuing down the leaf with fly stitch to the bottom. Work all of the small stems with whipped backstitch. Use two strands of thread throughout.

33. The larger stems, or branches, consist of two lines. Using two strands of thread, first work heavy

34. The large leaf comprises two sections.

- Using two strands throughout, fill the top section with basic trellis couching. Work the vein down the centre with heavy chain stitch. *Outline this part of the leaf with whipped backstitch.
- Still using two strands of thread, fill the bottom section with trellis couching with daisy filling (see page 47). *Outline this part of the leaf with whipped backstitch.

35. Work the branch that goes into the leaf, the branch below that and the branch that goes into the berry on the right following the instructions in step 33.

36. Work the leaves that come out of the main branches following the instructions in step 32.

37. Work the berry that comes out at bottom right of the large leaf following the instructions as set out in step 31.

41. Work the leaves that come out of the main branches following the instructions in step 32. The additional thinner stems that come out of the branches are worked with whipped backstitch using two strands of thread.

42. Follow the guidelines in steps 31 and 32 (see page 164) for these berries and stems.

43. Work this leaf following the guidelines in step 34 (see page 164). The stem going into the leaf is the same as step 33 with the heavy chain stitch worked on the lower line and the ordinary chain stitch on the upper line.

38. Start in the flower centre, using two strands of thread. Work a line of buttonhole stitch on all of the curved lines that depict each bit of the centre. It is best to start in the top row, dropping down to work one row at a time, making sure that the purl of the buttonhole stitch covers the raw edges of the beginning and end of the stitching in the previous row.

39. The petals around the centre of the flower are filled with trellis couching with triangular filling (see page 47) using a single strand of thread. When working the trellis, work over all of the petals as opposed to doing each one individually. Work the veins and outlines of the petals with whipped backstitching using two strands of thread.

40. Work the branches following the instructions in step 33 (see page 164) with the heavy chain stitch on the inside and the ordinary chain stitch on the outside of each branch.

48. Work all of the leaves and their stems following the guidelines in step 32 (see page 164).

49. Work the branches following the guidelines in step 33 (see page 164) with the heavy chain stitch on the left of the upward facing branch and on the bottom of the diagonally facing branch.

44. Work the centre of this floral motif with buttonhole stitch as in step 38 (see page 165).

45. Work the three outside leaves or petals following the guidelines in step 39 (see page 165).

46. Starting on the right, work heavy chain stitch on the line that divides the centre and the outside leaves along with the second shorter line from the tip with heavy chain stitch using two strands of threads. Work evenly-spaced French knots between the double lines on the right-hand side.

47. Now work the calyx leaves at the bottom of the flower using two strands of thread throughout.

- Work heavy chain stitch on the lines that define the inside sections of the leaves.
- Working with the dots that appear on the inside of the upper lines, place a French knot on the small dot and using the image above as your guide, work detached chain-stitch petals that radiate out from the French knot to create the impression of a small flower.
- Work ordinary chain stitch on the lines that define the outside of each leaf.
- Work evenly-spaced French knots between the double lines.

50. Using two strands of thread throughout, start with the thistle.

- Fill the main body of the thistle with trellis couching with daisy filling (see page 47), worked vertically and horizontally.
- Starting on the outside, fill the two spaces at the bottom of the thistle with buttonhole stitch making sure that the purl edge of the inside section covers the raw edges at the base of the outside section.
- Outline the main body of the thistle with whipped backstitch.

51. Work all of the leaves and the stems following the guidelines in step 32 (see page 164).

Templates

Claude (page 73)
Actual size: 260 x 320 mm (10¼ x 12½")

Colin (page 85)
Actual size: 310 x 280 mm (12¼ x 11")

Dave (page 105)
Actual size: 310 x 280 mm (12½ x 11")

Kevin (page. 119)
Actual size: 310 x 280 mm (12½ x 11")

Dick (page 135) – screen
Actual size: 290 x 290 mm (11½ x 11½")

Dick (page 135) – ripples
Actual size: 290 x 290 mm (11½ x 11½")

Dick (page 135) – composite
Actual size: 290 x 290 mm (11½ x 11½")

Nigel (page 155)
Actual size: 305 x 275 mm (12½ x 11")

Hazel Blomkamp has taught embroidery and beadwork in South Africa for over 20 years. She is the author of *Crewel Twists*, *Crewel Intentions*, *Crewel Creatures*, *Hand-stitched Crazy Patchwork* and two stitch guides – *Needle Lace Techniques* and *Needle Weaving Techniques*. She has also collaborated on *Freestyle Embroidered Mandalas* with Di van Niekerk and Monique Day-Wilde.

Hazel is a regular contributor to local and overseas publications and runs a busy website from home, providing embroidery kits and supplies to the four corners of the earth.

Travelling internationally to share her knowledge and promote her work, she is regularly invited to teach at international conventions. Her teaching has taken her to Australia, New Zealand, Western and Eastern Europe, North America and Asia.